PRAISE FOR *Counting Bones*

"Ellen Anderson Penno's memoir is an anatomy of precision and procedural beauty. *Counting Bones* takes the reader on a sure and steady climb, unexpected descent into loss, and through an ill-timed academic crucible. Anderson Penno pairs the rhythm and language of rock climbing with the nomenclative framework of Gray's Anatomy. In an introspective writing style that juxtaposes the creative with memoir Anderson Penno manages, in unexpected moments, to belay time, depart from the quantitative, and bring to light poetic concerns of the broken hearted."
DARCY TAMAYOSE, award-winning author of *Ezra's Ghosts*

"*Counting Bones* begins as a tale of a college romance rich with hiking, mountain climbing, skiing and the special sensation that comes from finding a soulmate for the first time but shifts into a complex tale of grief as a life-long visitor. The author loses her beloved to an avalanche on Mt. Baker in Washington just as she's finishing college and starting medical school. Her memoir reads like a symphony — an 'Ode to Grief' instead of joy, but just as nuanced and beautiful. 'Ian and Ian's death are like two different people,' she reflects, as the reader follows her through her complex reaction to the sudden trauma even as she faces the medical training required to handle trauma in others. If you loved Joan Didion's *The Year of Magical Thinking*, buy this book."
MARY COLLINS, author of *At the Broken Places: A Mother and Trans Son Pick Up the Pieces*

"*Counting Bones* is a book about grief told not obliquely, but head-on. With truth steady at her side and earth-anchored clarity, Anderson Penno masters the fine line between self-pity and self-glorification as she traces grief's path: the initial strike of near annihilating power, then its expansion to permeate all aspects of one's life before it begins to slowly, not lessen, but to shapeshift, transforming both itself and the writer. But *Counting Bones* is also a good story, a coming-of-age chronicle that will hold its readers as they marvel over the courage and resilience of an indefatigable, multi-gifted young woman."
SHARON BUTALA, award-winning author of *Leaving Wisdom* and *Where I Live Now*

Counting Bones

Anatomy of Love Lost and Found

———

COUNTING
BONES

———

·

Ellen Anderson Penno

NeWest Press

Library and Archives Canada Cataloguing in Publication
Title: Counting bones : anatomy of love lost and found / Ellen Anderson Penno.
Names: Anderson Penno, Ellen, author.
Identifiers: Canadiana (print) 20230455727 | Canadiana (ebook) 20230455794 | ISBN 9781774390924 (softcover) | ISBN 9781774390931 (EPUB)
Subjects: LCSH: Anderson Penno, Ellen. | LCSH: Grief. | LCSH: Bereavement. | LCSH: Ophthalmologists—Canada—Biography. | LCGFT: Autobiographies.
Classification: LCC BF575.G7 A53 2024 | DDC 155.9/37092—dc23

Editor for the Press: Merrill Distad
Book design: Natalie Olsen, Kisscut Design
Cover texture © Gosteva/Shutterstock.com
Author photo: Ellen Anderson Penno

NeWest Press wishes to acknowledge that the land on which we operate is Treaty 6 territory and a traditional meeting ground and home for many Indigenous Peoples, including Cree, Saulteaux, Niitsitapi (Blackfoot), Métis, Dene and Nakota Sioux since time immemorial.

NeWest Press acknowledges the support of the Canada Council for the Arts, the Alberta Foundation for the Arts, and the Edmonton Arts Council for support of our publishing program. This project is funded in part by the Government of Canada.

201, 8540-109 Street
Edmonton, Alberta T6G 1E6
780.432.9427
www.newestpress.com

NEWEST PRESS

No bison were harmed in the making of this book.
Printed and bound in Canada.   1 2 3 4   27 26 25 24

For Ian. Your memory is a blessing.

———————

CONTENTS

True grace is finding serendipity at the feet of chance.

PROLOGUE

August 3, 1986: car-sized blocks of ice fell from the Roman Wall on Mount Baker, Washington, crushing two climbers. One of those climbers was my first love Ian Kraabel. The article "Unburied: The Secrets of a Deadly Mount Baker Avalanche," published in *Seattle Met Magazine*'s April 2015 issue, detailed the contents of a backpack belonging to Ian's fellow deceased climber that had just emerged from the toe of the Coleman Glacier. A few months earlier a reporter had called me out of the blue, asked about the avalanche, and instantly transported me back to high camp where I kissed Ian goodbye for that last time in the predawn dark outside the tent before they left for the climb.

The *Seattle Met* article listed the contents in much the same way an anatomist records a dissection:

1 royal blue backpack lid

2 REI tags

2 sections of blue and yellow cord

1 toothbrush, toothpaste, and floss kit

1 tube sunscreen

1 vial cologne

1 crampon cover

1 headlamp and battery pack

4 AA batteries

1 snow fluke

1 blue mitten

2 lengths of 9mm spiral-twisted rope, ends frayed

1 Gideon New Testament Bible

1 Pentax camera, 1 roll exposed Kodak 35mm film

1 roll exposed Kits 35mm film

I was, at first, deeply angered by this list—even though it was not Ian's pack. How does this collection of objects begin to capture the loss of a life? If a bus runs me down, are the contents of my pockets—a crumpled receipt, half a granola bar, my wallet, and a safety pin—my lasting legacy? Are we nothing more than the things we carry?

On the other hand, these last objects do harbour clues to the owner's habits or frame of mind. Pondering this list reminded me of the text *Gray's Anatomy,* a whole book of lists. Henry Gray published the first edition of *Gray's Anatomy* as a young man in 1858.

This seminal text is a methodical framework for medical students to use when learning human anatomy, and is still used more than a century later. I purchased *Gray's Anatomy* at age twenty-four, in first-term medical school, just weeks after the 1986 avalanche. Decades later, while leafing through the yellowed pages of a 1917 edition of *Gray's Anatomy* from the rare book collection at a medical school library, I understood that my memories could be dissected in exactly the same way. This list of last objects unburied after three decades is just like a catalogue of cadaver parts. In both cases lists are only one part of the truth, but I realize now it's a place to start.

PART I

THE SKELETON

*the bones
of the story*

JENNY, ELLEN, AND IAN GOOFING AROUND ON THE STEPS
OF THE ANDERSON FAMILY HOME SUNWOOD.

fig. 1–1

THE RIBS

---

the rib speaks of love and healing

"Cows, Colleges, and Contentment" — that's how it started. I met Ian in Northfield, Minnesota, where all visitors entering the town were greeted with a large sign emblazoned with this motto. Stately golden sandstone academic buildings, nestled into pastoral woods, projected long shadows onto adjacent cornfields. Westerly winds carried the comforting scent of Malt-O-Meal, while easterly winds were steeped in the musty, less pleasing aroma of turkey farm. Ian and I both enrolled in Carleton College, a small liberal arts college in Northfield, I from just two hours north in 1980 and Ian from Seattle in 1981.

After Ian arrived on campus, our paths crossed frequently in the green space at the centre of campus on our way to and from classes. As a small college with a total enrollment of about 1600 students, we bumped into each other on the periphery of various groups, each acknowledging the other with a studied laissez faire. We met officially in 1981 when members of the combined downhill and cross-country ski team were introduced one by one by the captains at a team meeting.

Why I caught Ian Kraabel's eye, I don't know for sure, but I know exactly why he caught mine. He moved with compact grace, had thick, dark, curly hair and snapping ocean-blue eyes with crinkles in the corners, and he was always on the lookout for adventure. All the world was simultaneously his playground and his classroom. He had a gravity that attracted people, as if he were the sun in his own universe, counterbalanced by a keen ability to savor each moment. "Flying down the mountain" was downhill skiing alongside Ian; he brought intensity and ease to every action.

The son of a French mother, with a strong Catholic heritage, he also channeled a love of family and a romantic view of mountains and of the Alps in particular.

"My name is pronounced 'yawn' — you know, like you're tired," he patiently explained to each new person he met. "It's the French pronunciation, not the English."

That first fall, I noticed his smile and athleticism. He would lounge on the steep grassy hill in the shade of Evans Hall, a big, old, red-brick dormitory offset by painted, white, wooden window casings, while casually leaning on one elbow, a book or notebook open in front of him, ostensibly studying while I played field hockey on the flat playing fields below. It was hard to concentrate with him up there on the hill watching me.

I didn't wear a field hockey kilt, but instead sported sweatpants, goalie pads, and a mouth guard. I tried not to notice him on the hill and to concentrate on the task at hand, which was to stop all incoming balls. My coach Eileen would line up the field hockey balls on the half circle line chalked on the grass in front of the goal, just a few feet away, and face me. I lay on my stomach, field hockey stick in hand, toes on the goal line, face towards the row of hard plastic, fist-sized, white balls at eye level through the blades of green grass. Then Eileen would hammer balls towards me at various angles.

"Hit!" she barked each time she swung her stick.

I had to jump up to stop each ball before quickly lying back down again to prepare for the next shot. The team all knew that Eileen wearing her glasses meant she had a migraine, signaling that today's practice would be particularly taxing. She would not take any less than the best you could give. As a result of her coaching, I was a good goalie, or maybe I have rewritten my memories to make it so.

"I'm so disappointed you don't get to wear a cute skirt like the rest of the team," my mom lamented the first time she saw me in goal.

"These goalie pads are much better than a kilt. They make me look bigger," I replied. "So I can do this," I roared, holding my arms up, stick in hand, posing like an angry bear, startling her.

"I see," she said, laughing.

Ian and I spent most of that fall term observing each other, he from the hill at my field hockey practices and games, or when both of us competed at the combined downhill and cross-country ski races, or when passing by on the grassy commons. Sometimes we saw each other at the computer lab that housed rows of work terminals, the ghostly green blinking icons just waiting for the next student. I noticed him and, apparently, he noticed me, but we were never formally introduced. Throughout the winter of 1981–82 I heard about Ian's wins on the slalom courses and watched him tune his slalom skis in the waxing room, using old electric irons to melt the wax. I can still smell the vapors of the various combinations of ski wax he used. I always caught the scent and knew what snow conditions were being prepped for, based on smell alone, before rounding the corner to the waxing room.

By the time Ian arrived for his freshman year, my sophomore roommate Jenny and I were already best friends. Jenny was my best pal during those years, and still is. She has been my alpha and omega to the decades that have passed, as solid a foundation to my soul as are the bones to my body. She continues to be a singular golden thread in the tapestry of my life, among all the other lovely threads that are the people whom I have gathered over these many years. We mostly have lived thousands of miles apart, not communicating for months, yet she is always there to pick up as if we just spoke yesterday.

Jenny and I met during the orientation week in 1980, the year before Ian arrived. That first night on campus we attended the minority freshman mixer, not because we were part of a minority, but because she felt strongly about social justice. We became great friends, then roommates, then travel companions. Her nickname for me was "Ellie-Mae" which was better than my childhood nickname of "Elly-Belly". One day as we walked down Main Street in Northfield our elbows bumped.

"Our auras are attracting," she said. "It must be because we're both Geminis!"

"Oops—there I go again!" She bumped me again. "I'm such a klutz."

And then she laughed and bumped me again. I smiled, thinking so far the college experience wasn't too bad.

Carletonians (not to be confused with students at Carleton University in Ottawa) prided themselves on individuality and uniqueness. In the 1980s, this meant we ranged from the preppy in docksiders and pleated khakis for the men and bows in the hair for the women, to the football and hockey crowd, to the stoners and loners; we were like high-school cliques put in a blender, the result of which was a fluid mix-and-match vibe where booty shorts or bow ties would all be considered appropriate for lecture-hall attire. In this context, Jenny's aura comment was right on target.

"The girl I sat next to today had the distinct odor of a long-haired, guinea-type pig," she rambled on. "And the creature who runs around in my innards agreed."

I laughed with her.

"And then I got myself ever so lost on the way back from class..."

Jenny was an early bird to my night owl. When we roomed together, she would already have been up for hours by the time I finally rolled out of bed. Most mornings, she was tucked into a chair cuddling a book, leaving a trail of balled-up tissues in the cushions of the various reading chairs she inhabited. A trait shared, I've noticed, with my present-day ophthalmology clinic patients. Her laugh sounded like a bellow if she really got going, in contrast to her usual quiet manner and small stature—you could hear her across the dinner hall or two rooms away. After Carleton, she gravitated to religious studies and eventually went to divinity school to become a Congregationalist minister.

I have boxes of letters Jenny sent after she moved away to Vanderbilt University in Tennessee, some written on the back of photocopied poems, postcards, cartoons, and scraps of fancy paper. There are letters written on the very thin, overseas airmail paper that would save on postage, letters written on placemats, and some decorated with ink-stamps or pasted-on cartoons; letters from Jenny and mixed in with Ian's letters, tucked away for decades in shoeboxes in the closet. From time to time, a new letter still appears in my box; her tiny, cursive, run-on sentences and fragments that read like poetry spill into the creases of the paper, over the top and around the corner to cover every inch. Most recently she mailed me a set of waterproof laces, I suppose for my hiking boots, and a small army knife "to cut through all the crazy." She is my personal e.e. cummings. Many words and not too much punctuation have built and maintained a thirty-five-year conversation between us that has waxed and waned, but never ended. Now that we're digital, she randomly texts me with happy thoughts like, "Hello friend, I just wanted to let you know that I love you and I think you are great." And I do the same since she's a kindred soul.

Although Jenny has mostly been far away since our Carleton days, our words and our shared history continue to connect us. I still have a framed eight-by-twelve, black-and-white photo of Ian in his classic red-plaid cotton, button-up shirt sitting next to me in my white-wool, cable-knit sweater on the steps of my parents' old house—Jenny sitting one step above, one arm around Ian, the other around me, and laughing.

As the months passed following Ian's arrival on campus, I was aware of my increasing attraction to him, but somehow the more attracted I was, the more shy I became. We never spoke directly to each other that year. When the academic year came to a close, we all went our separate ways, Jenny to Michigan and Ian back to Seattle. That summer of 1982, I got a job as a maid at McKinley Park, Alaska, which was later renamed Denali Park. Shortly after I moved into the staff housing a letter arrived care of Denali National Park — I didn't know that Jenny told Ian where I would be that summer:

> *Dear Ellen,*
>
> *I feel a (more than) little sheepish writing you this letter. But what must be done must be done. For case you hadn't noticed, I have a crush on you. Yuck I said it, what a sappy thing. But anyhow who could blame me, you're a very interesting girl. Hardly being a "Lance Romance",*
> *I felt a little akward (however you spell that) when you left. In the back of my mind I was hoping to let you know that I thought you were a neat person and wish you a good summer in Alaska. No big deal. Only (you looked as though you would have decked me if I had said anything)*
> — that line was crossed out in the letter but still legible — *you didn't look very receptive after that final so I kept my trap shut. Well you've left and I still hadn't said anything which I regret. I'm sitting around regretting it rather than doing my paper and it is getting on my nerves. So I decided to write you and say: Ellen I think you're neat! Have a good time in Alaska.*
> *— crushedly yours, Iano*

Reading that letter gave me exactly the feeling that I had on a ski trip at Sun Valley, when I rode up on a chairlift with Clint Eastwood. I surreptitiously tried to stare sideways at Mr. Eastwood from behind my wraparound glacier glasses, determined to play it cool. Mr. Eastwood is tall and looked just like he had stepped off the movie screen. At the top, as we readied our poles to head toward the runs, he asked, "How are the back bowls?"

"Oh, you know, if you've skied one you've skied them all," escaped my mouth. At which point the voice in my head said, "What the hell, Ellen! How stupid can you sound?" I quickly skied away to disappear down the slopes, having lost my capacity for intelligent speech.

Faced with this "crushedly yours" letter, I was flooded with a mix of my star-struck heart fluttering, frustration that he hadn't said anything before we left campus, and a what am I supposed to do now deer-in-the-headlights feeling. Having nowhere to flee to, I promptly ripped the letter to pieces. Within minutes I taped the letter back together using clear cellophane tape. There was no internet and no long-distance calling plans, and I had no idea how to respond to Ian's admission having never actually spoken to him, so the rest of the summer months passed without comment.

Once back on campus in the fall of 1982, Ian showed up at my dormitory door.

"We should go down to Grundy's Corner Bar for a beer," he stated, our shared knowledge of the crushedly yours letter hanging between us.

"Okay," I replied simply, blushing.

So off we walked the few blocks down the hill, through the sleepy streets of Northfield to the classic, downtown, corner bar on Main Street. We settled into the smooth, faux red-leather booth seats, the tall, dark, wooden backs created a sense of seclusion in the busy bar. Conversations and laughter of people at other tables blended with the clink of bottles, the swoosh of beer being drawn from the taps, and the commentators on the football game on the television in the corner, blended into a blanket of sound. Resting our hands on the worn wooden table, we sat together under the watchful eye of the giant, tacky painting of a naked lady reclining on a red-velvet chaise who presided over the barroom with an almost smile, like Mona Lisa's racy third-cousin. We talked into the night over pitchers of cheap, draught beer.

Between planning his next climb or ski trip, Ian devoured books like *Gödel, Escher, Bach: an Eternal Golden Braid* by Douglas Hofstadter. While driving he'd morph into Speed Racer, the main character of the late 1960's Japanese cartoon known as Mach 5 GoGoGo. He loved the anime series that involved a race car driver targeted by gangsters. As Speed Racer, Ian, knuckles white, clutched the steering wheel of my tan '78 Chevette beater I had named Murray that sported worn, orange and yellow, racing stripe decals, pushed in the clutch to rev the engine, "Hang on Trixie, looks like a reckless driver."

Reaching for the "holy-shit" handle above the window, I hung on as he slid his hands back and forth along the wheel pretending to swerve back and forth, imitating the best car chase movies like *The French Connection*.

"Watch out, Speed, you're over the limit, and we're supposed to obey the law," I pointed out, laughing.

"Whew, that was a close one," he would say, looking back over his shoulder at the imaginary bad guys. "Good thing we've got the Mach 5," he'd add, patting Murray's dashboard.

He would also randomly grin and point to his flexed bicep saying, "Blue twisted steel, it's the strongest material in the world."

"Urban myth," I'd say.

Blue twisted steel was part humor and part truth. Although slim and not tall, Ian was lithe and strong. And purposeful. A habit from his mountaineering experience, he always found the most efficient walking routes across campus, which mostly meant cutting across the grassy lawns or jaywalking diagonally through an intersection, maneuvers he called "hypotenusing". I adopted this habit, and it has stuck with me and been shared to subsequent friends over the past three decades — we continue to hypotenuse.

He borrowed another saying from mountaineering. "Never gain unnecessary altitude," which meant walking around instead of up and over any vertical obstacle such as stairs in a city or a hill or ridge in the wilderness. Ian gathered experiences that combined creativity and intensity to fuel his next endeavor, like a hurricane gathering strength over warm ocean waters.

Ian excelled at downhill skiing and I at cross-country skiing, so Minnesota snow provided our first common ground. We both spoke snow, but different dialects. I acquainted him with the upper Midwest's minus twenty degrees Fahrenheit to plus forty lake and flatland variety. I knew the very cold snow below zero, fine like dust, too cold to have a scent, and the corn snow after a late winter thaw that has the consistency of gravel and a smell like wet dog. I knew that clouds sometimes look like snow, the air promising frost, and sun dogs around the sun or moon warning of rain or snow coming soon. I had camped out on the thick lake ice, deep enough to drive trucks on, and observed the mysterious cracks that disappear into darkness; the icy mass sang to me in random creaks or snaps when I listened long enough.

As a December baby, the month when new snow covers the landscape like a giant sugar bowl sparkling past the shortening day, Ian embraced winter. Even though he was from the West Coast, he'd travelled in search of snow. He introduced me to the capricious alpine snowpack and the inscrutable language of glaciers.

You know, as soon as I think I know ice and snow from top to bottom I learn something new. Even now, especially when I'm thinking about Ian, I learn new lessons. Recently I hiked over the frozen Abraham Lake in Alberta where naturally occurring methane gas rises from the lake bed to create a myriad of shapes and bubbles in the ice, forms I had never seen before. Standing on the ice in the middle of Abraham Lake and looking down through the cascading frozen bubbles into the deep black of the water beneath, I thought of Ian. He would have appreciated this oddity and would have delighted in trying to puncture the bubbles to light the gas on fire. Snow and ice equal opportunity.

As Carleton students we all took ourselves way too seriously, aspiring to live up to the ivory tower to which we had been admitted. From science to philosophy to political science, I delved into deep conversations with Jenny and Ian along with my fellow students. In this playground of intellectual possibilities we all believed we could live up to these lofty Socratic pursuits.

There was the concept of "soulmate" that we discussed at length. We took very seriously the notion we were academics, so tried to draw on the classics whenever possible. We discussed Plato's *The Symposium* that describes mythical human creatures who were female-male, female-female, or male-male, and could travel quickly by rolling around on four arms and four legs.

"Makes sense that Zeus struck them all in half. That's what I would do if I were a Greek god and they were disrespecting me," was Ian's take.

"Well you aren't a god, and I'm not a goddess. But that seems so sad. All those single halves wandering the earth in search of their soulmates."

"But also, nice to know there's someone out in the world for each one of us, even if you never find them."

"What if you never find your other half?"

"You can have fun looking."

Such a romantic idea, only one true love. This feeling that you must be in fact a part of the other. Eve made from Adam's rib, for instance. Because being madly in love feels like you must be meant just for that one other person. Or have been in a former life a part of that person's life. There are myths older than Adam and Eve in which the rib embodies connection and healing. Enki the Sumerian God of water was also the keeper of the divine powers of *Me*, the divine decree essential to the development of human civilization. His spouse Ninhursag, Lady of the Mountain, heals Enki through his rib. These are tales of love so deep that you would give a part of your own body in order to heal your partner, no matter the stakes.

Maybe romantic soulmates are real, but I have decided, perhaps out of necessity, that you can have more than one. I am sure that

Jenny and I are platonic soulmates. We still joke about being old ladies taking trips on the bus after we can no longer drive. Perhaps Eve had a female pal made from her own rib. Oh, and a beautiful part of this scenario is that under the right circumstances human ribs can regenerate, which leads to endless possibilities.

HATCHING PLANS FOR THEIR NEXT ADVENTURE, IAN AND ELLEN
IN HER DORM ROOM AT HALL HOUSE, CARLETON COLLEGE.

fig. 1–2

THE HAND

---

thankful for touch and strength

After our first date at the corner bar, we spent many hours over the next few years in the Carleton College arboretum, the "Arb" (about eight hundred acres of land), running, walking, and skiing through the hardwood forest along the wide dirt trails. In spring we found secluded, fragrant, grassy meadows among the oaks and maples, to lie down together in the warm sunshine.

We were packed and ready to go downhill skiing in Montana over spring break that first year we were together, and right before we got into Murray for the fifteen-hour trip, I farted.

"Oh my god, I'm so sorry," I gasped.

Ian laughed. "Get in — I'll open the windows."

For some reason we had a cassette tape of the Guess Who featuring "American Woman", a decade old at the time, that became the theme song for that trip. We stayed in a basement apartment of a friend in Bozeman, and because Ian was a few inches taller than I, he bumped his head nightly on the basement air vents, swore, but then forgot to duck the very next time. That vacation was the only time I've seen my name in lights, thanks to the "Ellen" theatre in downtown Bozeman.

"To the Roundhouse, Mabel!" Ian would yell, raising a gloved hand to point ahead, regardless of what mountain he was skiing on, as he sped down the cat-track on the way to the day lodge; the Roundhouse is a day lodge at Sun Valley, Idaho, but I have no idea why he addressed this joyous shout to Mabel.

On this trip, we skied Bridger Bowl and Big Sky, with a side trip to Red Lodge. Since we were living on student loans, we carried lunch in a daypack on downhill ski days, stowing it in the snow towards the top of the hill for a mid-day meal. On sunny days we nestled together in the crisp snow, munching our sandwiches. The mountain expanses unfolding before us gave way to broad valleys with distant, opposing peaks rising on the horizon. Our white-bread sandwiches with thinly sliced salami and crispy iceberg lettuce were almost always smushed flat, but my mouth still waters as I remember eating them, cozied up to Ian at the top of the slopes. The smell of sharp winter air, fresh snow, and sunscreen still conjure that stunning scenery on those perfect ski days.

Snippets of my time with Ian pop into my head, and make me laugh even now. I see an image of Ian's silly toiletry kit that he swiped from his father and brought up to base camp on an alpine trip in the summer of 1986; he doused himself with awful smelling cologne so that he would smell good for me at the end of the week. Apparently, he didn't realize I preferred the scent of sweat.

Another snippet: Ian parallel parking Murray in an impossibly small spot in Chicago by lightly tapping each bumper against the cars in front and back until he had squeezed our car into the spot, about one inch to spare on both ends.

"That's what bumpers are for," he proclaimed, duly proud of his parking job.

During our second year at Carleton, 1983, Ian confessed to having a hometown honey. He told me he had been seeing her over the summer while he was back in Seattle and I was in St. Louis for a summer laboratory internship. I was disappointed, although this hometown honey scenario was very common at a college where every summer students scattered back across the country to their home states. Many high-school friends and honeys stayed in their same hometown lives, so some students got into the habit of shuttling back and forth between these two lives.

"She makes me nervous," he confessed. "I feel like a rat abandoning a sinking ship."

"Well, you'll have to choose," I told him.

"I told her I can't go out with her," he said. "And she told me she's been seeing another guy for a while anyway, and she says he's more her type."

He went on to talk about regrets he had about spending so much time with her during high school to the exclusion of other friends and activities, and that he felt much more at ease with me. He had broken off the relationship, although he said they were still friends. After a lot of talk and tears, I decided to trust he was telling me the truth.

Ian introduced me to rock climbing in those early years. We did a lot of traditional climbing and top-roping, which means we would hike to the top of a cliff, set a belay, in which the rope is secured at the top with anchors, then toss the two ends to the bottom. A standard climbing rope is sixty meters in length (about 197 feet), so theoretically you can top-rope a climb of eighty to ninety feet if the belayer is at the bottom.

At the top of the cliff above the climb we planned to do, we used chocks — metal wedges on the end of wire loops in various shapes and sizes designed to be slotted into crevices in the face — followed by carabiners which are sturdy metal clips to secure the chocks to loops of webbing to set an anchor. The nylon webbing strips are made of synthetic fiber in colours from red and blue to brown or earthy green, and slung together with carabiners through which the rope slides freely. We also had *friends* — cam devices that can be retracted to fit through a smaller opening, then released within the right-sized fracture in a stone face to provide a strong anchor point.

We always set three anchors, sometimes using large sturdy trees and chocks or friends placed in suitable cracks in the cliff. As the sport became more popular, climbers started to set permanent bolts with clips on select routes so that climbers did not have to set their own anchors.

Once the rope was set, we'd hike down to the bottom, then one of us would climb and the other belay. The climber secured one rope end with a knot like a figure-eight to the harness, and the belayer used a device such as a Grigi breaking device, or ATC (air traffic controller), to provide a mechanical advantage with friction in order to be able to freely draw in rope as the climber ascended, while at the same time maintain a position to quickly lock off the other end of the rope if the climber were to fall.

"On belay?" I say once my harness is secured to the rope.

"Belay on," Ian confirms.

"Climbing," I announce.

"Climb on," he confirms.

With a top rope, the climber should not fall more than one or two feet, making it possible to tackle more challenging routes safely. With lead climbing, where the lead climber places the rope while moving up the rock face, the climber could fall up to twice the distance from the previous anchor, and bigger falls increase the potential for injuries. Once at the top of the pitch, a pitch being roughly a rope length, the lead climber sets anchors to belay the following climber, who then cleans the route on the way up, gathering all the anchors, although sometimes it is harder to remove one than to set it.

A favorite destination of ours during the Carleton years was the rocks at Taylors Falls along the St. Croix River on the border between Minnesota and Wisconsin, about twelve miles as the crow flies up-river from Marine on St. Croix where I had spent my junior-high and high-school years. In the St. Croix river valley where the cliffs rise up above the river, a canopy of deciduous and pine trees provide deep shade in summer and fiery red, orange, and yellow colours in fall. There are numerous routes in among these cliffs, with names like Piece of Pie, Piece of Cake, Lunge or Plunge, and Fancy Dancer. Sometimes we set one rope to climb a few routes, other times we climbed just one before moving to a different spot, all the while enjoying the scenery and the challenges each vertical path presented.

Climbing has its own rhythm and language, with routine cadences to maximize safety, including the starting "On Belay?" sequence. "Up rope" or "slack" are words that need to be understood and acted on; if the climber and belayer are on opposite sides of a corner, a muffled "blah-blah" means "up rope" and a single-syllable "blah" means "slack." An experienced partner can tell from the movement and tension on the rope if the climber may need slack or a tighter belay. Climbing requires teamwork for safety and efficiency, so most climbers will gravitate toward a partner they get along with well. A new partner or careless partner can be terrifying. I was always in good hands with Ian.

Often, early in the morning, we'd have a climb to ourselves in the majestic solitude of rocks, river, and forest. On those cool mornings, a veil of mist hung like a pearl necklace over reflections of the rising sun on the still water. Rock climbing is usually done in dry conditions, since wet rock is treacherous, so only a light drizzle can be tolerated. Depending on the contour, the rock face can sometimes provide shelter to those below, although it may also pose a hazard due to a possible rockfall. On a sunny weekend as the day went on there might be a halt to allow the climbers ahead to finish the route because only one climber can do a particular route at a time, so we'd wait for them to finish before setting up for our climb of that route. Spectators would give "beta" to the climbers; *beta* meant "advice" and came from "Betamax," the original video-tape format.

I stayed in Northfield one year after graduation in 1984, to work in a biochemistry laboratory and assist in coaching the field hockey team, while Ian completed his senior year. After Carleton, in the summer of 1985, Ian moved back to Seattle to pursue his dream of becoming a mountain guide. He had not yet finished his comprehensive senior project, "comps" we called it, which was a major paper required for him to earn a BA as a history major; he intended to work on it over that summer.

Like most of the students who graduated before us, that summer Jenny and I backpacked for three months across Europe—it was almost a rite of passage in those days. All of us knew this was our time to travel, to expand our horizons. Most of us didn't really know what would come next; it was our time of uncertainty and exploration, the natural next step in our post-Carleton lives.

Letters from Ian arrived for me in Germany and Greece, and he always said hello to Jenny, inviting me to share his letters with her. The letters were frequently several pages long and sometimes written over many days, like diaries. In one letter that summer he wrote:

> *I love you. I realize that we may not be seeing each other forever, and that's been a sort of damper on letting me express my feelings towards you. But now I realize that the uncertainty of what is to happen between us is not an excuse for hiding my feelings, but the contrary. No matter what happens you'll always be very special to me. Shit, I'm no poet Ellen, but I love you and knowing you has made my life a lot better.*

I felt sure that we would somehow end up together in the same place after all our adventuring was done.

After months of travel, Jenny and I moved together to Vermont where I cross-country ski raced and worked as a waitress and at a downhill ski shop at Sugarbush resort. Ian and I continued our written communications through letters and postcards.

Hello! Hello! I wrote to Ian in September 1985, just before mov-ing to Vermont. *And hello from Jenny too. We have worked ourselves into a fine nervous frenzy as suddenly our lack of money and jobs strikes us in the face of our impending move to an unfamiliar state...* I am sad to read that you loathe the future [a reference to an earlier letter from Ian to me] *when to me it is an exciting maze of possi-bilities — of course I am the one who loves to plan and plot so am excited by such a nice opportunity! I think you have things to do with your future but are just unsure and unused to a lack of structure — face it, you had little choice but to go to school for seventeen years and nothing but a summer to deal with. Also your fear of 'Adult Life' — who says we have to espouse 'Adult' 'Mature' attitudes and lifestyles? How boring...so be excited for yourself — look into your ideas, research, learn, look around. So what if most of it doesn't lead to employment or money, look at each new idea as a potential for providing you with something you need or want; not necessarily material either... so Iano, this misplaced lecture can be put away until you need it.*

Vermont felt colder than Minnesota, greasy snow coating the roads, the slippery slime a different dialect of snow altogether. One December day in 1985, I made a serious error in judgment. I was with a co-worker from the ski hill. Having driven Murray — far too light and old for this kind of weather — past my turn so I decided to make a U-turn. The road was crowned, which means the centre is higher than both sides, as most roads in the north are to prevent water from collecting on the surface and freezing. In this case Murray's turning radius came into adverse relationship with the crown of the road, and I was pointed dangerously towards the deep ravine just past the edge of the ditch. There I was, sideways to an oncoming car headed down the ice-covered road, with the steep ravine at my front bumper on the downhill side. In high school I was in a winter accident in an AMC Pacer where we rolled into a wooded ravine, so I had a vivid memory of ending up in a car upside down. But this time there was also the risk of being broad-sided.

"Oh shit! Hurry—get out and push," I told my passenger.

"On it," she said, jumping out to push the front.

Rolling down the window, I yelled, "Okay—ready? One, two, three." Then I put Murray in reverse, revving the engine and waiting until the last second to fully release the clutch. Because Murray was very light, my co-worker was able to push the car back far enough to complete the poor choice of a U-turn on a slick road in Vermont before the oncoming car slid into us.

I told Ian that near-death story when he called that night. We had started having phone conversations once I had a stable landline. Later that same week I called again to tell him, "I frostbit my big toe today skiing and the tip of it turned black. Funny how you don't remember sensations like the pain of frostbite until—ah yes, it hurts."

"Ouch," he commiserated.

It was just a hazard of skiing in the freezing temperatures, to be expected for those who live in winter, and familiar to both of us. I was in the habit of not taking my socks off until I could feel my toes, afraid of what they may look like. Although I knew this would never happen, I worried that a toe might have just broken off, and it would be horrific to take my socks off and see that one was missing, black like a frozen jelly bean, loose inside the toe of the sock. The stages of almost frostbite are first numbness, which makes the digits feel like someone stuffed a bunch of pickles in place of toes, then burning as warmth creeps in, toes on fire, and finally the toes returning to the body as if coming home after a holiday. And then I could take my wool socks off.

Before one of my cross-country ski races, Ian had flowers delivered to me via the Mooselips bar and restaurant where I waitressed. All the while we continued to correspond with our letters and postcards and some long-distance calls in between. In those days the long-distance calls were expensive, so we tried not to phone too often.

By late 1985, Jenny was making plans to take her Masters in Divinity degree at Vanderbilt. I had been accepted to medical school at the University of Minnesota for fall, 1985, but had deferred it for a year to travel and explore. My year would be up in ten months. I was to start medical school in September, 1986.

Jenny and I spent Christmas in Vermont, the first time either of us had been away from our families for the holidays. I came back to our drab apartment on Christmas Eve to find she had baked something — an amorphous, tan mass like a stain on the cookie sheet was cooling on the counter, a whiff of burnt butter hanging in the air.

"What is this shit?" I said.

"It's peanut brittle," she replied with pride.

I picked up a piece, stuffed it in my mouth, and promptly broke my tooth. Served me right, I guess. Somehow we found a dentist in that small Vermont town on Christmas Eve who kindly fixed my tooth. Jenny and I also pulled up a very tiny pine tree from the forest, roots and all, for our very own "Charlie Brown Christmas tree".

In spite of the expense of long-distance, Ian and I had several more telephone calls as the year turned over to 1986, exploring the idea of moving in together.

"How can you be sure you love *me*, and that you're not just in love with the idea of being with someone?" Ian asked.

"How can you expect me to parse that out? How much is you and how much is having a companion. All I can say is that I know that moving to Seattle feels like the right thing to do right now, and that I am pretty sure that it is the actual you and not the idea of you that I am in love with," I replied. "You are the one who told me that love is a verb, an action, so I am choosing to act, to love, to move to Seattle." We finally agreed that I would, in fact, move to the west coast.

"You can't date my brother or my climbing partner," was one of the first things he told me upon my arrival in Seattle in early February, 1986. "Even if we were to break up," he added, to be clear. Both brother Brett and climbing partner Dave were fit and handsome young men, and had I not been so fiercely loyal to Ian, perhaps he would have had cause to worry. But there was no question for me that it would not be an issue — love of family and friends was the earth beneath our feet, and had been for both of us long before we met.

Dave, who had been Ian's climbing partner for several years, echoed Ian's explanation of how to pronounce his name.

"Yawn. It's yawn, you know…like you're tired? Or if you prefer a lively roll of the tongue — Iano! Truly a unique sound," he explained. "It carries as well in the mountains as it does from his mother's back porch. There is an energy unleashed when one gives out a good yell of Iano."

Dave and Ian both loved the mountains, and in his mountains Ian was at his best.

The three of us went climbing in the Cascade Range where the routes involved hand jams and finger jams. Hand jams were a favorite of mine. This is a technique where you cup your hand like a beauty queen wave and then jam it into a crack in the cliff face, palm on one side of the inside of the crack and the back of your hand wedged along the opposing side; you then pull yourself up on your jammed hand. A finger jam is another technique that involves positioning your fingers almost as if you are about to snap them, then jamming your digits into a smaller crack in the rock. With these moves it is possible to hang your body weight off your fingers or hand in order to move your feet to the next position—then hands then feet, then again hands then feet—and like climbing a rope you make your way up the rock face. Each route was a challenge in deciphering the craggy rock faces that always remind me of the faces of old men and women.

We taped our hands to prevent the skin from scraping off from the friction, which did not always work; the backs of our hands mostly looked like scraped knees. To improve grip, we used chalk powder like that used by gymnasts to stick our skin to the stone walls. Chalk and sweat mingling together is the signature scent of rock climbing that evokes the thrill of standing at the top of a cliff. For me it was a scent better than any perfume or cologne. Memories of these climbs trigger phantom soreness of hand and forearm muscles. It was hard even to turn a door handle the day after a long route. These memories bring back the feeling of expanses of air and space, of hanging off a rocky precipice, becoming one with the landscape and sky.

Dave and I went to Castle Rock and it was one of those dream days where everything went so well it seemed like I was look-ing through the lens of a movie camera, Ian wrote about one of their climbs.

As a climbing partner Dave held Ian's life in his hands, and as long-term friends they shared a history of adventures and dreams. Dave had a good sense of humor, and a cool, vintage, white Dodge Dart in mint condition, with the exception of the ability to reverse. Creative parking, as in making sure there were no obstructions in front, or parking on an uphill slope so the car could roll back with gravity, would usually do the trick. If he had a couple of passengers, the passengers would hop out and push the car to reverse.

One summer day at a small general store somewhere in the Cascade mountains, Dave parked in the usual front-forward manner because Ian and I were with him, so pushing the car back out would not be a problem. We got back into the car after our trip into the store, and just at that moment a Washington state trooper pulled up and parked right next to us. It seemed likely that not having a reverse gear might be illegal, so the three of us sat in the Dart while the trooper went inside. When the coast was clear, we quickly opened the doors and put our legs out to walk the car backward with our feet like Fred Flintstone; luckily it was easy because of a mild incline. Tucking our feet back in, we slammed the car doors shut just as the trooper exited the store. Perhaps the trooper knew full well what we were all giggling about as we drove away.

Dave recounted a hike they'd done a previous year, the northwest ridge of Mount Shuksan; the route chosen for purity of line, spectacular scenery, and safety from objective danger, all qualities that he and Ian never disagreed about. Objective hazards are risks — such as the ice fall off the Roman Wall on Mount Baker or a rock slab peeling off a cliff above — that may happen at any time without being triggered by the actions of the alpinist. When routes traverse areas of hazards the goal is to pass through quickly to minimize risk. That said, nothing was more satisfying for both men than a route that demanded all their mountaineering skills, even a nasty bushwhack through difficult, heavily forested terrain without a trail, or delicate route finding. Their favorite routes had a mixture of snow, rock, and sometimes ice. Careful and precise planning was a requirement.

According to Dave, Mount Shuksan had it all. Two thousand feet up the side of a heavily forested ridge, they'd had to battle the bushwhacker's best friend, the Devil's Club, a shrub with sliver-sized needles that can inflict nasty wounds. They climbed half the ridge in the cool evening, then it started to get dark.

As they put on their headlamps, Dave looked at Iano and said, "I don't know anyone else stupid enough to do this."

Ian looked back at him, blue eyes crinkling, "That's why I'm doing it with you!"

It turned out Ian had convinced Dave that the route demanded travelling light; in fact, at the car, he had talked Dave out of bringing his sleeping bag. That evening, when they finally reached base camp on the route up Mount Shuksan, Iano pulled out his favorite red wool sweater that must have weighed four pounds dry. That four-pound red sweater was a favorite staple on our trips to the mountains. Ian had taken over the article of clothing from his father Paul, then I took it from Ian. It is enormous, fire-engine red, and made of wool that takes on both heat and weight if it gets wet.

In Dave's bivi sack was a simple cloth covering, which just isn't the same as a cozy down bag. He was cold all night, delighted to get up at three AM for the summit attempt. As they climbed Ian and Dave always chatted, especially enjoying a good debate. Their go-to debate was regarding the ice axe. The ice axe, shaped like a miner's pickaxe with a point at the end of the shaft, is a mountaineer's standard tool. At the head of the axe is a short, broad, flat blade on one side—called the adze—and a longer, serrated, curved pick on the opposite side. Ice axes vary from fifty to seventy-five centimetres long depending on the use and the height of the user.

"The axe should always be carried in your uphill hand, so you have better stability and a quicker arrest on deep snow," Dave insisted.

"Your dominant hand will always be stronger, which means you won't be trying to do an arrest with your weaker side," countered Ian.

Both methods are acceptable, but that was never the point. Each was determined to convince the other to abandon his position entirely. This, of course, never happened, so the game went on. Nothing was more satisfying to Dave than to catch Ian using his uphill-hand method, and nothing satisfied Ian more than seeing Dave use his dominant hand.

The weather on Mount Shuksan that particular morning deteriorated, forcing them to turn back, not an easy decision since it meant reliving the Devil's Club bushwhack.

"Shuksan wasn't nothin' to mess with if she didn't cooperate," Dave later admitted, full of regret.

They retreated back to high camp just as the weather cleared. They'd been tricked; it was too late for that ascent. But it says a lot about their endurance and persistence that they were successful in conquering Shuksan the following year.

That spring, after we moved in together, Ian and I concentrated all our energies on adventuring and making enough cash to pay rent. To have cash I had to have a job. My undergraduate BA degree in biology was not worth anything to the restaurants and coffee shops that I'd applied to daily for the first couple weeks in February.

"These espresso machines are very expensive," one shop manager chastised me after I admitted to having no experience making coffee, "We can only hire people with experience."

I guess my prior summers of running centrifuges worth many thousands of dollars and setting up electrophoresis gels in the biochemistry lab did not qualify me to learn about brewing espresso.

After a brief stint as a door-to-door saleswoman handing out free thermometers and pushing a local health insurance product, I finally landed a cashier position at a small grocery just around the corner from where Ian and his mother were living. Shortly after that, we found the Lake Union apartment, also within walking distance of the neighborhood store.

After we moved in together, Ian often left me notes. One read, *I want your body…*written on the outside of a small folded scrap of paper and on the inside revealed *— to go climbing with me this weekend — Iano.*

One climb I especially remember doing with Ian was called Outer Space. According to the guidebooks, the whole point of climbing this route is to get to the main crack and enjoy every hand and finger jamming move, my favorites. Another feature of Outer Space is the Chicken Heads along the route. These are rock formations like a series of doorknobs, perfect for hand and footholds.

It was a brilliant, dry day, and the clanking of our gear as we approached on foot put us in the mood for the ascent. Ian was the more experienced climber, so he mostly led, then set a belay for me to follow. Typically any route requiring a rope will be rated on a 5.0 to 5.15 scale. Easy climbs will be between 5.0 and 5.7, intermediate to hard from 5.8 to 5.10. Anything above that would be extremely difficult. The top of Outer Space was an easy 5.0 rating, so I led the final pitch. Having only been the lead climber a few times, it was still exhilarating and a little frightening for me. Each time I set a piece and then climbed above it I was conscious of a potential fall twice that distance. It was an uneventful lead until the very top. As I crested the cliff a large white mountain goat was standing just a few feet away from the edge. As startled as I was to see him, he looked at least as spooked, and stared steadily at my face as I peeked up over the edge of the rock face. Seconds stretched as we eyed each other. Taking a breath, I contemplated a down climb, and calculated how far I might fall if the goat chose to charge me. Ian was out of sight belaying me from below. He would have no way of knowing what was happening unless I yelled down to him, which I did not want to do for fear of startling the goat into becoming aggressive. After what felt like forever, the goat ambled away. I imagine I looked pretty small and non-threatening with just my head poking up at ground level, and from my lower vantage point he likely appeared much bigger than he really was. In the end there was a successful finish to the goat versus girl standoff at the edge of the cliff, and the encounter provided a memorable end to a stellar climb. I pulled myself over the edge with strong tanned hands, and as I yelled "off-rope" to Ian from the top of Outer Space, I felt pretty *neat* indeed.

IAN, AKA "SPEED RACER," BEHIND THE WHEEL OF MURRAY
(ELLEN'S TRUSTY CHEVY CHEVETTE) LOADED UP FOR A SKI TRIP OUT WEST.

fig. 1–3

THE FOOT

---

step, rest, step, rest, repeat, repeat, repeat

The windows in the living room of our one-bedroom, Lake Union apartment in Seattle faced Yale Avenue. We painted all the walls white, refinished the oak floor, and bought a patterned oriental rug in shades of deep red, navy-blue, and white, just like the one in Ian's mother's house. The tiny galley kitchen in back of the living room had a gray metal table for two positioned by the window with a partial view of the Seattle Space Needle. The kitchen also served as the hallway to the small bedroom, just big enough for a double bed with a two-foot clearance to the miniscule washroom that was about the size of an airplane bathroom.

Our carefree tangle of bodies would have me sleepily confused as I awoke, my hand resting on his stomach, thinking it was my own body I was touching. Interwoven together in the warm blankets as the sun came up, mornings were my favorite time. We were almost the same size and even had the same size feet. Our clothes were mixed together in drawers and closets.

Our routine every workday was to roll out of bed into the kitchen to share a bowl of Grape-Nuts and a cup of coffee across the small table. As we crunched our cereal, we looked out towards the Space Needle to gauge the skies. Our only weather app in those days was to look outside. Weather forecasting was critical for planning trips to the mountains, and that spring Ian had taken a job as a bike messenger downtown so rain made the difference between an enjoyable day and a miserable one. Ian liked to choose physical jobs like landscaping and the bike messenger gig so that he could become stronger and spend more time outdoors while earning a wage, always with the intention to be as fit as possible for climbing, mountaineering, and downhill skiing.

After breakfast, we drove Murray the short distance downtown, where I would drop Ian off at the messenger office. Every morning, before he got out of the car we would give each other a kiss.

"Love you!" And he would shut the car door and head into the office to pick up his bike route as I drove away. I parked back at the apartment, then walked to the corner grocery, to my cashier's job just a few blocks away. My path took me under the looming highway overpasses, which offered the quiet cool shade of a concrete cavern. After working a month, I got to know the customers at the grocery, not by name, but by the products they purchased. At exactly the same time every day the same man rounded the street corner, and appeared in the large front windows of the store.

"A package of Kools," he would drawl, slapping his money down on the old wooden counter. Before long as soon as I saw him at the end of the street, I pulled out the package of Kools and had the cigarettes waiting for him beside the till. He still always smacked his cash on the counter and drawled, "A package of Kools." On my walk home, a couple of times a week, I bought fresh flowers from a woman who had a cart with an array of tulips, daffodils, carnations, and irises in the shadows of the highway bridges.

Sometimes Ian and I went out for beers with Dave or other friends at the local pub and sometimes we stayed in and lay together on the patterned wool carpet in the living room to talk. Our go-to argument was whether it would ever be possible, given an infinite amount of time and resources, for science to prove or disprove the existence of God. We were no theologians, but were steeped in our Catholic upbringings, yet casual about attending church except at Easter and Christmas.

"That's a ridiculous idea." Ian was emphatic that science could never shed light on God. "There is a reason it's called faith."

"Just to be the devil's advocate, pun intended, how can you be so sure that there aren't physical properties that might be discovered that would prove there is a God?" was my stock reply. "Disproving God is the more difficult problem."

Around we would go, lying on the carpet in the living room, neither of us reaching a conclusion, nor expecting to. A line from Madeleine L'Engle's *A Wrinkle In Time* reminds me of Ian's argument.

"Well I know Charles Wallace is different, and I know he's something more, I guess I'll just have to accept it without understanding."

That is what many call faith, accepting without understanding. The irony of that book is that the characters push for the use of science and math to understand things that appear impossible or magical; in the story they succeed in discovering the tesseract, the method to transcend both time and space, which supports my argument that it is possible that science may in the future explain things that we cannot yet understand. But the point of our debate was not to win, but to discuss in depth, possibly increasing our own understanding in the process.

I had not yet heard about the Celestial Teapot, Bertrand Russell's analogy to question why the burden of proof should lie with the person claiming the reality of God rather than the burden of disproof falling to the non-believer. Russell argues that he might claim there is a tiny teapot in space orbiting the earth too small to be detected by our terrestrial telescopes, and he should not expect anyone to believe that such a teapot exists without proof. In the early 2000s, another satirical concept was floated by the religious activist Bobby Henderson who wanted the teaching of religion to be kept out of schools. He invented the Pastafarian Church of the Flying Spaghetti Monster; the question, much the same as the Celestial Teapot question, was who can say there is not an invisible, undetectable, Flying Spaghetti Monster that created the universe? I know Ian and I would have had a lot of fun debating both the teapot and the monster.

After finishing classes in 1985, Ian worked sporadically on his comps paper, the final requirement for his undergraduate degree. He was as deeply drawn to history and philosophy as he was to the mountains, but the mountains always seemed to win out.

If only I could capture everything—youth, potential, actualization, death—I could write a story perhaps, he told me. *It would be the story of a man who tries to make a living from his passion and in the attempt to mix the real and the dream, he destroys both.*

I told my shrink about how I feel forces are pulling me in differ-ent directions — comps, mountain climbing, passion and purpose, freedom and responsibility, he continued, leaving the topic of the two of us, our relationship and its place in all this, unaddressed. *I told him nobody ever said I had to do everything at once and he just said, "So you're looking for someone to tell you the importance of being patient."*

We left notes to each other on the kitchen table, the bed, the dash of the car. *Mistress Suzzallo is cracking her musty whip,* Ian wrote to me in one, as he was pushing to make comps progress. This was a reference to the main library at the University of Washington where he would go to write. Another time he clipped out a cartoon from *The New Yorker* and left it for me to find; it was an ink drawing of a dog patiently sitting outside academic buildings and a scholar telling the dog something like, "I'm sorry I can't play right now, I'm working on my PhD." He had my name written over the dog and the word "sorry" in black ink in his familiar, curly, condensed hand-writing that was a combination of cursive and printing.

The previous year, shortly before we decided that I would move to Seattle, Ian wrote this in a letter:

Well here I am sitting the library with sore muscles again.
Sort of sums up my existence doesn't it? I went skiing
yesterday. I'd tell you about it but I'm sure that by the time
you receive this you'll have heard all about it on the phone.
So instead I'll tell you about the problem of hindsight. It's
a problem which plagues all historians who seek origins of

a particular event, be it the French Revolution or why the Royals won the World Series...The problem with hindsight is that once you choose the explanation of a certain event as the goal of your historical research, in my case the separation of Europe into two religiously associated camps, you are forced to look at the period leading up to the event through the lens of that event. And that leads to descriptive distortion. Because you're looking for a cause, that's how you must describe the earlier period, as a cause of event x, thereby ignoring the countless other potentialities inherent in the situation. Consider for comparison's sake the period of turmoil most college students go through shortly before or after graduation. They are torn by conflicting desires: future employment and feeding themselves today, maintaining relationships with distant friends and yet allowing themselves enough flexibility to take advantage of the unexpected, enjoying life for the moment and leaving their mark on the world. If someone were to approach a young person at this stage in his life and tell him that in reality what he was experiencing was the origins of his career as an insurance salesman and his marriage to his college sweetheart, that person would most likely be told to go to hell. Not for lying, but for being so insensitive to what was going on at that time in the student's life. Historians in search of historical origins run the risk of a similar fate.

Ian's parents separated while he was at Carleton. It was tough on his whole family. I am not sure of the course of events, but one summer between spring and fall terms he went home to his mother's tiny new apartment to find he had no bed or dresser; he had to sleep on the floor and live out of a suitcase. That may have been the same summer he grew a beard while in Minnesota. In Seattle his mother gasped when she saw him, his brother Brett laughed, and his dog Jasper wouldn't stop barking until he shaved it off.

One day in early 1986, we went for a walk on Queen Anne Hill near his father's new place. Ian stomped back and forth across a low wall at a park overlooking the city.

"I am so frustrated," he ranted. "I have no sense of belonging like I did before my parents separated."

I shadowed him, walking next to the wall on the grass. Not having had to deal with divorced parents I could only provide a supportive ear.

"I'm sorry. I wish there was something I could do," was all I could offer.

"My dad approaches things as though it's all a math problem. He really does mean well, but the real problem is that he refuses to address, namely, my state of mental and emotional well-being. I know that if I was feeling positive myself, I would crank out my comps. But my dad is not one to discuss anything distressing..." Ian trailed off. I can still see him pacing in silence in the waning light on Queen Anne Hill overlooking downtown Seattle.

It was a complicated time and a simple life. There was no solving the math of his parents' divorce, nor finding a simple formula to set out our path forward. The future, between the two of us, was unspoken. Medical school was right around the corner for me; we knew that, yet we chose to focus on our daily chores and our weekly challenges—hiking, climbing, or mountaineering were absorbing enough to push even the near future to a distant horizon. Navigating a rock face or glacier demands full attention, tasks perfect for avoiding harder choices.

By June we had settled into our jobs, our apartment, our work, and our mountain routines. We didn't make a formal agreement not to talk about the future, but the future *was* in the future; as the months stretched into summer it felt right to concentrate on routes and gear, to plan no further than our next trip.

Just before my birthday in June, I woke up to an empty apartment and a colourful bouquet on our tiny kitchen table; a penned note on a ruled page torn from a notebook read, *To my little flower with a big sense of adventure. I hope you enjoy these kiddo—love Iano.* I looked out the window to the street just in time to see Ian driving up with two sea kayaks lashed to the top of Murray. The peeling, yellow racing-stripe decals on the sides and a smattering of rust were a nice contrast to the colourful kayaks. Ian had arranged the impromptu kayaking and camping trip in the San Juan Islands for my birthday.

The night before we left, we spread out all our gear across the rug in the living room. We sorted, packed, and planned. The galley kitchen and tiny bedroom and bathroom in the apartment were much too small for pre-adventure organizing, but the living room had plenty of space to lay out all our equipment, clothing, and food—since we both favoured outdoor gear over furnishings.

Staging our gear was a pre-trip ritual, whether our adventure was climbing, hiking, skiing, or kayaking. Depending on the trip, we might have day packs or larger overnight packs, hiking boots, crampons, tent, sleeping bags, cook set, water bottles, ropes and climbing hard-wear, bug spray, sunscreen, fuel bottles, and a mix of dry and fresh food including our favourite Fig Newtons. Fig Newtons are the perfect pack food, sweet and dense enough to withstand being crushed into a backpack and tasty no matter if frozen or smashed. Other food staples were bricks of cheddar cheese that sweated on hot days, trapped in their plastic packaging, and salami sausages that we sliced using our Swiss Army knives to savour no matter how greasy the meat got in the heat. That night in the apartment, we lit the WhisperLite camp stove for a short time to ensure there were no gas leaks or plugged tubing. Headlamp and flashlight batteries were tested, and extra batteries stored in Ziploc bags. Sometimes we'd set up the tent in the yard or in the living room to check that all the parts were still in the tent bag, but we didn't that time.

Methodically lining up all our items for a check and double-check, we packed contents according to weight and accessibility to provide the best balance, while keeping the most frequently used items in the top or side pockets of the packs.

We were a team in our preparations, whether for Ian and his climbing partner Dave, or if Ian and I were planning a trip together. We shared the purpose of meticulous organization. The longer the trek, the more important it is to pack your backpack properly. Outerwear, footwear, and socks were selected for the specific journey; in 1986 wool was the go-to material for socks and inner layers to hold heat even if water-logged, because everyone knows that "cotton is rotten", a saying that captures the discomfort of being caught in the rain or wet snow in a soggy cotton sweatshirt. For the San Juan kayak trip, shorts, flip-flops, and tennis shoes would do. After all our preparations, we sat on the carpet together to share a beer and admire our work in anticipation of yet another outdoor adventure.

As night fell on our campsite, it was as if the stars had fallen into the Pacific Ocean that June night. Shoulder to shoulder, bare skin to bare skin, toes burrowing into coarse, still-warm sand, quiet waves murmuring in the twilight, we were transfixed by the phosphorescence glittering in the sea. Bioluminescent plankton formed an aquatic aurora borealis that danced within the slow tide. Our twinned breath relaxed to the rhythm of the water and the scent of well-earned sweat lingered after a long day of kayaking. It was a perfect start to my twenty-fourth year.

In early summer, Ian and Dave decided to offer themselves as mountain guides. They developed the specifics of the plan after several conversations that winter. It was not a surprising choice to make their idea a reality, given their experience, physical fitness, and long obsession with climbing. They adopted the name "Summit Mountain Guides," and produced a glossy, fold-out brochure with black-and-white pictures of local mountains and the tagline "Picture yourself at the top of a major Northwest peak." The several climbs offered included Mount Shuksan, Mount Baker, Glacier Peak, and Eldorado Peak for $50 per day per person. Guiding had a long history in Europe, it but was only in the late 1970s that North American mountain guides were more formally organized, so Ian and Dave were in tune with current trends.

Ian's goal was to gain experience guiding in Washington State and use that experience to connect with bigger companies, then someday get certification to become a guide in the Alps. His ideas were big and fuzzy.

"When I finish my history degree, someday I might want to be a prof at a place like Carleton," he mused.

"Someday like after you're tired of guiding?"

"Who knows, but it would be nice to ride my bike to work and spend the day talking about history to kids who are interested."

"I can see you now in an old brown corduroy blazer, with worn-out jeans, tooling along on an old single-speed bike," I told him.

Summer was drawing to an end by late July, and so was our living together for the time being. There was no question that I would be starting medical school in the fall, and I imagined that just as we had weathered many months apart when I went to St. Louis, travelled in Europe, and lived in Vermont while he was back in Seattle, we would weather the next year and eventually end up in the same place. This was my equally fuzzy idea—a different version of having faith.

Ian and Dave were still doing climbs, just the two of them, without clients. With no cell phones, in those days we just made a plan estimating how long a climb would take and what time we could be expected to get home. Mostly that worked well, but Ian and Dave were badly late one evening after a climb on Mount Rainier; there was no way to know where they were or why they were delayed.

Mountaineers have to register to climb at Rainier so the park rangers know who is on the routes at any given time. If climbers don't sign out there may well be a need to start a search—fortunately not a very common occurrence. I assumed they had registered and checked out. I also knew that the rangers kept rough track of the climbing parties. I still sat in the living room by the window overlooking Yale Avenue for hours that evening, long past the time Ian was supposed to be back. I watched the sky darken as night overtook the city street. I told myself to stop being such a worrywart.

Finally, Murray pulled up in front. When Ian entered the apartment I hugged him hello, but did not share how upset I had been.

"The hike out took longer than expected, but otherwise it was a
great climb," he told me as he unpacked his gear. He was tired, but
happy and relaxed. He was already sorting his gear in the living
room for the next trip, his lateness no big deal to him in the scheme
of things.

In the final days of July 1986, I tagged along with him on a
guided trip to summit Mount Baker. At 10,781 feet, Mount Baker
can be seen from Seattle and a number of other towns and cities
in Washington state and British Columbia. It attracts experts and
novice climbers alike. An active volcanic peak in the Cascade
Range, it juts skyward from the surrounding landscape with stunning altitude. Wilderness areas, like those in the Casacades that
are hard to reach, beckon climbers with a promise of true solitude
in nature, but bagging a peak also comes with the dangers of rock-
falls, avalanches, and crevasses. If you've experienced climbing
to the top of the peak that can be seen outside your window or
in picture postcards, you will understand the allure of conquering peaks. Prehistoric remains preserved in glaciers attest that
our early ancestors traversed mountain ranges. And ever since
Horace-Benedict de Saussure decided to climb Mont Blanc in 1760,
people have yearned to reach peaks that had yet to be topped.
Mountaineers work hard to reach that point from where they can
gaze down knowing they have, under their own power, navigated
that vertical path, to be rewarded with this unparalleled view. What
an accomplishment. Once you have reached one summit it becomes
harder to resist the jagged spells of others.

To climb Mount Baker takes in the neighborhood of 30,000
steps, each step increasingly difficult with altitude gained. Walking

up a mountain is time consuming, in part because the steep sections require a climber to pause before every step to breathe, the pause allows oxygen to reach the screaming muscles in one's calves and thighs, as oxygen becomes thinner on each upward advance. Mountain climbers deliberately kick their crampons forward and down, driving the teeth into the snow to ensure a secure footing. The lead climber creates packed footprints for the others to follow. This is called a "rest step," a technique Ian taught to me and his clients. As in all things difficult, sometime that pause is critical.

This was our second to last Mount Baker trip. After the usual training day, practicing ice-axe arrests and crevasse rescue techniques, we woke before dawn and took the popular Coleman-Deming route, which affords stunning views. The weather was clear and sunny, but despite multiple applications of sunscreen, one client got a severe sunburn across her nose and face that took several days to improve. It was otherwise an uneventful trip, a success. The guiding was working well so far, and another group hired Ian for a Mount Baker ascent the following week.

PART II

THE BLOOD

a little bit of blood goes a long way

TAKING A BREAK DURING A CLIMB.

fig. 2–1

THE HEART

---

breaking, bleeding, beating

We hiked up to base camp on Mount Baker with three young clients, Kurt Petellin, Steve Raschick, and Tom Waller, under sunny skies. Powering up the trail with new companions, full of the optimism of youth, our talk centred around how heavy our packs were, the equipment, and the weather forecast. Ian and I had our usual collection of gear and clothing, much of it second-hand. I wore an expedition-style, tan wind shell that had passed, like many other items, from his father Paul to Ian and then to me; it was ridiculously too big, but windproof and good for layering underneath.

A few new pieces graced our wardrobe, including a burgundy, North Face pack that I was very excited to have purchased brand new. It was a technical pack with an internal frame, outside pockets, a removable top piece that could be used as a separate small pack, and expandable sides with a zigzag cord to shrink or grow the pack as needed. For this trip the new pack was expanded to its fullest, with fresh fruit and wine adding extra pounds. Ian carried an additional ten pounds of food. We knew carrying the weight would be worth the payoff at dinner. Some dehydrated meals taste like dog kibble or sawdust, and real food and wine taste even better at altitude. High camp is at approximately six-thousand feet at the end of the winding path through shaded pine forests along Kulshan Creek at the foot of Mount Baker. It normally makes no sense to carry extra weight, but on a multi-day trip, with a couple nights at high camp, it made sense. The final steps of the approach lead over a dirt trail out onto the dazzling treeless ridge below the glaciers and snow-covered upper mountain.

High camp, also called base camp, is usually an area at the highest altitude that can be reached without ropes and technical gear, from where climbers are in position for the early-morning ascent over the icy terrain above. Our high camp was stunningly barren, allowing a panoramic view of blue skies above and pristine white down below. Rocky outcroppings like sentinels divided the safety of our plateau from the jaws of icy cracks that riddled the Coleman glacier cascading down the valley beside our encampment. There was a gentle incline nearby that would serve as a classroom for practicing ice-axe arrests and crevasse rescues.

We pitched our tents on a level area with fine, brown, pea gravel underfoot, not too close together but close enough, in a friendly grouping overlooking the Coleman glacier on the shoulder of the magnificent summit. Mount Baker, known as Kulshan in the Lummi language, is always cloaked in a white robe. The upper mountain was criss-crossed with craggy features, furrows resting under the dome of a cloudless sky, the puzzled ridges considering the forested slopes sashaying below to the base of the mountain. The mountain air was clear and perfect under a beautiful sunset.

Mount Baker features the most heavily glaciated terrain in the State of Washington. This makes it an alluring choice for climbers looking for the archetypal mountaineering experience, and close enough to Seattle to be a popular target for guides and their clients. Glaciers hover in ravines, hanging in seracs over ledges like frozen fingers slowly clawing off the leading edge of sharp cliffs, and deep cracks disappear into dark depths without visible end. Formed from a compacted river of ice that hangs on the side of mountains, glaciers move slowly, taking years to reach lower altitudes. Like ice in an old freezer that spills off the ice cube tray from cycles of thawing and freezing each time the door is opened, so it is with glaciers. Through the decades of daytime heat and nighttime cold and changing seasons, gravity relentlessly pulls down the thick ice, dirt, and rocks. Freezing, thawing, compression, and flow create snow and ice fields fractured by deep cracks called crevasses. Fractures, sometimes hidden by snow bridges created by surface snowfall, can be more than a hundred feet deep, all creeping in location over time as the icy mass slides down the mountain.

We spent that day at high camp training, and practicing the ice-axe arrests first. The adze should be forward and the pick facing back, one hand on the top of the shaft, usually secured by a short leash around the wrist. As the climber falls, the free hand grabs the shaft and the axe is drawn up to the chest with two hands; the pick facing down should act as a break as it digs into the snow. Lifting up one's feet is advisable to avoid crampons catching, which could cause a climber to cartwheel or injure their legs. Self-arrest with an ice axe is a serious technique that can save lives, I liked training day on these guided climbs. It reminded me of sledding as a child in Minnesota: a bunch of children or young adults sliding down a snowy hill with no risk of danger, only to end up in a snowball fight. After several climbs up to slide down again we lay down in the warm sun on the softening snow to rest.

The other skill we practiced was a crevasse rescue using Prusik slings, thin cords tied to the climbing rope with Prusik knots — hitch knots that work by friction — to form slings. Alternating one's weight on the slings allows them to be moved up or down, to climb up or descend by a rope. There are various techniques to anchor the rescuer and each climber has two Prusik slings: a short, waist Prusik and a longer foot sling. The rescuing climber ascends the climbing rope by stepping on the foot sling to unweight the waist Prusik so it can be moved up the rope, then sits in the climbing harness to put weight on the waist sling, then slides the unweighted foot sling knot up the rope, alternating the two slings. There are variations in using the Prusik slings, but the basic technique is the same.

Ian and I shared one tent for the two nights at high camp, our three fellow climbers slept in their own tent. Murmurs from the other tent, vocal cadences wafting through nylon walls, reminded me of being a child upstairs in bed listening to the grownups downstairs. Ian's planning gave us ample time to unpack the stove and food, reorganize our gear, and cook our fresh food over the Whisperlight gas stove. He was in fine form, methodically checking and lining up boots, packs, ropes, down to the smallest details like glacier glasses and sunscreen. The rest of us buzzed around the tents, fueled by anticipation of the climb. Because I had summitted

Baker the previous week, I decided to hang out at base camp while Ian guided the others up to the summit. I was content to provide support by preparing food, cleaning dishes, and checking gear.

That second night at high camp, the night before the ascent, I dreamed Ian was walking between two bottomless crevasses, then he fell into a crevasse and died. I got up with him at just a couple hours after midnight, and told him about my dream before he left for the climb. I did not ask him not to go.

"Don't worry," he told me and kissed me. "I'll be back around 2:00 p.m."

For reasons I do not recall, they decided to take a slightly different route up the Roman wall to the summit. Northern Lights danced across the sky that still night. It was surprisingly warm. The Aurora Borealis is named after the Roman goddess Aurora who rides across the sky in her multicoloured chariot each night with her purple cape flowing behind her to usher in the dawn. The moving lights are electromagnetic waves in the atmosphere, more common in Northern skies. Although I had seen them in Minnesota numerous times, I had never seen them in the mountains before. The sky above Mount Baker that August night was sparkling with magic, like the phosphorescent tide we had shared on my birthday eight weeks earlier on the beach in the San Juan Islands.

"Maybe I should join you," I almost said.

But since I hadn't prepared my pack and equipment the night before, I felt I shouldn't delay the rest of the climbing party, since an early start is a necessity for safe climbing. In truth, I was less intent than Ian in bagging peaks, content with our simply spending time together in the outdoors. I stayed quiet and helped to make sure everyone was well prepared before setting off. According to the custom and wisdom of climbing mountains, Ian, Kurt, Steve, and Tom set out in the very early morning hours, the middle of the night really, to avoid the thawing snow and ice in the afternoon. Sun warms the surfaces of snow and rock, and temperature differentials between the outer layers and the cooler depths can lead to rock and ice fall and avalanches. Well before dawn, on August 3, 1986, Ian and his three companions stood together in a little group.

"Goodbye. See you in the afternoon," I said, after a final kiss goodbye.

"Love you."

Off they marched into the dark with headlamps, like trains in a tunnel, crampons noisily crunching the cold snow with rest steps in a steady rhythm. Step. Rest. Step. Rest. Repeat. Repeat. Repeat.

I crawled back into the tent and fell asleep. Always a vivid dreamer, from a family of vivid dreamers, I was not usually superstitious about them, but that earlier dream was hard to shake. I awoke again at sunrise to poke my head out of the tent into the sunshine, and my eyes were drawn to a rough patch on the mountain that seemed to be on or near the route I knew they were taking on the Roman Wall. I tried to talk myself out of worry.

"They're okay." I said aloud to no one. "They'll be fine," I continued, trying not to study the route above me.

In retrospect it seems likely that after going back to sleep, I must have heard the rumblings of the avalanche in my unconscious, perhaps that was what woke me up. Avalanches heard from far away sound like a giant pouring dried breakfast cereal out of a box. Trailing rocks and ice ping-pong in the aftermath like stray toasted oats bouncing off the counter to roll across the kitchen floor, the whole movement reverberating off surrounding cliffs. If you are quiet in the mountains long enough you will hear a rock or ice fall, just as when you are on a frozen lake in silence you will hear the ice speaking. Repeating to myself that everyone was okay, I roamed around the campsite making coffee, folding and refolding the few extra clothes we had in the tent, and tidying up everything two or three times.

Helicopters arrived over the horizon a while later, like large ominous insects piercing the quiet, to hang over the alpine meadows. Helicopters are a synonym for disaster. This news was bad. I walked a hundred yards up to the next base camp to find out more. I knew my heart was broken, and I knew I just couldn't feel it yet. I knew. Identities were not confirmed, so I tried to push these thoughts out of my head.

"Four climbers, avalanche, search and rescue…" Various campers had parts of the story.

There was nothing to do but go back to the campsite, putter around to try to stay busy, periodically looking up at the Roman wall, at that rough spot I cannot unsee, hoping that my heart was wrong. It was not wrong.

The campsite was above the treeline, so it was impossible not to be aware of increasing activity on the snowfields above. I tried to concentrate on making more and more coffee, and rearranged the tent yet again. It was midday by the time a rescuer came to the base camp. The approaching figure, as I expected, confirmed that it was my party that had been involved in an avalanche. He let me know that there were two missing, two injured and flown to hospital. Ian was missing.

It was a warm clear day. It seemed important to me to walk back down that mountain. I had walked in with all my gear the day before. It wasn't right that I would not walk back out on that lovely summer day. But the rescue personnel insisted I be flown down in a helicopter.

August 3, 1986 was my first helicopter ride. Loud and high. Thumping of blades and scratchy radios. Snatching me off the mountain in spite of the fact I was not in any real danger. We floated up and away from the mountain through the windless sky. White noise enveloped me as Mount Baker receded beneath us like the white foam of an outgoing tide.

HIGH CAMP.

fig. 2–2

SURFACE MARKINGS

---

evidence of buried truth

They took me to a ranger station, where I was dimly aware of the staff in the office offering me the telephone. I called Ian's parents in Seattle, but could not reach his father Paul.

What is the right way to deliver bad news? I know now what not to say.

"I hope you are sitting down," were my first lame words to Ian's mother.

In my shock I apparently only had the capacity to speak in clichés. Ian's father was a Seattle city councilman, so the avalanche immediately became the story of the day. His father ended up finding out from a reporter that Ian was missing. Paul later wrote in his self-published memoir of stories and poems:

August 1986: I was alone in my apartment on the Crest of Queen Anne hill when the phone rang. It was a reporter I knew from the Seattle Times who led off with, 'Are you the father of Ian Kraabel?' — words you never want to hear. Ellen was his girlfriend who was camped up on the side of Mt. Baker with him. On this day, Ian was to guide a party of four up the mountain. Ellen stayed behind. There occurred a very minor earthquake, felt by virtually no one (but registered on seismic records), which knocked the cornice off of the top of the mountain. . .resulting in the avalanche.

The avalanche was described in newspaper accounts as a wall of ice that came crashing down at approximately 8,800 feet on the Roman Wall, ripping the harness off one climber and burying two climbers in a crevasse.

From the ranger station, a nice man, whose name I don't recall, drove me back to Seattle. My only recollection from that drive is suddenly having to pee, so he had to stop the car at the side of the road while I scurried across the ditch into the bushes. No other details of that drive stuck with me. I was not able to notice anything other than my own internal struggle, trying to understand what was happening, forgetting to breathe. The road seemed long and quiet. Like a bear going into hibernation for the winter, I mentally circled inwards to my core, suffocating in disbelief. I felt like I was underwater, sounds muffled, everything around me drifting away. I had the driver drop me at my friend Lynne's house once we got back to Seattle, to make more calls to let people know what was happening before it was all over the news. Even so, the media rush to report the accident did not allow our families to inform one another in a gentler way; the media was a swarm of fire ants feeding on our tragedy.

Lynne's telephone was a crazy replica of a 1920s candlestick telephone with the rotary dial at the base, a black tower type of thing, and a goofy speaker at the top to talk into with a separate listening piece attached by a wire.

"Don't you have just a regular telephone?" I asked, faced with the ridiculous contraption.

I needed a plain old telephone with the comforting smooth plastic handset, receiver, and speaker together in one place to grip with one hand, preferably black, connected by a friendly familiar curly plastic cord to the base, with an ordinary rotary dial. She did have a regular telephone, and I was able to make my phone calls. I believe I called my sister Meg in Minnesota so that she could pass the news to my large family, not having reserve enough to call everyone. Then I called Jenny. I asked Jenny to call any of our friends from Carleton she felt would want to know about Ian being missing, hoping to stay ahead of the news outlets. Language gave me away. I immediately started speaking in past tense, although the search and rescue was ongoing and everyone was talking about hope.

"Ian was—I mean is…" I kept saying.

I will call it "word dysphoria." Although no such disorder exists, it should. What is the word for "may be dead but not for sure but probably is but shouldn't think like that because must have hope and hope it is not true"? Unfortunately, I had no hope, and I felt guilty about that. That thread between life and death is very, very slim and fragile, stretched to the breaking point by the searching after a loved one is lost. In those moments the task of managing past versus present tense was equivalent to climbing a major glaciated peak on a unicycle;

my inadvertent verbal transgressions into past tense carried a heavy load of guilt each time I spoke. Of all Ian's people, I should have the most hope, but hope cannot be fabricated. My language was the truth.

Even though it was not the right time, I immediately started my period, bleeding from the shock of death. That and urgently needing to pee on the way home from the mountain stick in my memory. If only my body could have had the courtesy to suspend regular bodily functions for a while, that would have been nice. Instead I felt I would die too, all my fluids draining out after the hand of fate had smacked me with a wicked backhand. It took massive willpower to put one foot in front of the other like a zombie, the alternative being to fall on the ground and wail.

The day of the avalanche, after rescuing the two surviving climbers the search was temporarily suspended due to the softening snowpack and unsafe conditions for the rescuers. The following day, Ian's family gathered, and we went up to the staging area when the search resumed. A yellow police tape line cut across the dry dirt road on a ridge across from the Roman Wall, Ian's family on one side, reporters with cameras trying to push in on the other. We waited to hear a report from the searchers. Tan dust swirled up among us in the rising heat, the staccato beat of helicopters circling punctuating the scene. I was hopeless, but tried to put on a hopeful front.

"We have no reason to believe that the lost climbers will be found," we were told by Whatcom County Deputy Sheriff Tim Ortner. "We don't like to do this. This is the part of my job I don't like, but there are people who have been up there since 1917. There are airplanes up there from the Second World War,"

Ian's father Paul thanked the rescue workers, voice quivering, "There are four families that would like to thank the mountain rescue people. They've been wonderful."

My mind was sucked into the black hole of loss. I only vaguely remember that two of my sisters had already flown from Minnesota to Seattle to join us on the mountain. My lovely family dropped everything to support me, and I can barely remember exactly who came or how long they stayed.

Monday August 4, 1986 the *Seattle Times* carried a large photo of the rough spot, the avalanche below the Roman Wall, and the surface markings of the trauma below. "Little hope of finding climbers," the bold headline screamed from the front pages of the papers.

At 10:30 a.m., according to the *Seattle Post Intelligencer*, "just as the sun was beginning to bear down over the Roman Wall" the officials broke the news to the families.

"Hope is slim, and rescuers are clinging to a thread," the Whatcom County acting director of emergency services Dave Jenkins was quoted saying. "He was such a tough bastard, I thought for sure he would survive," Ian's brother Brett remarked.

"Hope Abandoned on Mount Baker," proclaimed the headline on the front page of Tuesday's *Post Intelligencer* beside a large photo of Ian, looking classic Ian in his old gray jacket and black watch cap with an old-school, hemp rope coiled over his shoulder, pensively staring off to his left as if considering his next adventure.

All that was left of Ian was one torn rope at the edge of the crevasse, with only part of a seat harness remaining. Ice — reportedly thirty feet deep in places — was strewn over an area the size of a football field with some chunks the size of cars. The snowpack left from the avalanche was as dense as cement. There was no possibility of using probes to look for the lost climbers. The search canines found no scent. There was nothing to be found.

"No one in their right mind would want to stay up there."

NO MONEY, NO WORRIES. LIVING ON STUDENT LOANS,
IAN STILL FOUND A WAY TO GIVE ME FLOWERS.

fig. 2–3

THE CAVITY

---

falling through nothing

"The line between life and death is carelessly drawn and easily erased." This sentence by Susan J. Brison, from *Aftermath: Violence and the Remaking of a Self,* (an article that Jenny sent me) elegantly sums up the feeling of floating along the edge of existence that results from a sudden death or trauma. For the few weeks remaining in August 1986, I was stranded in the in-between; in between youth and adulthood, in between trauma number one, Ian's death, and trauma number two, the glacial and relentless trauma that would be medical school and internship, in between Ian's death and finding his body. I was neither here nor there. I did not yet know my grief.

Ian's siblings, parents, and I gathered on his father Paul's homey houseboat after the search was called off. Lake Union was still and beautiful under blue skies, sunshine washing over the planked decks beside the cheerful wooden house, its white trim smiling down. Mount Baker kept her victims, forcing a service without Ian's body. His family and I sat on the deck talking and taking the occasional swim. Recalling actual conversations is impossible, my memories are soundless, like early twentieth-century silent movies. Visuals stutter as if projector gears were catching on damaged film. The depths of the lake called to me, a dark silence I willingly jumped into, going limp to drift down into the quiet cool depths, sunshine fading above, air bubbling up and away; but no matter my intentions my lungs sent me gasping to the surface each time.

During those first few days most of my large family flew out from Minnesota, gathering for the funeral. My family was present, but separated from me by the pain of loss that might as well have been a pane of glass, isolating me in my sorrow. The memories of the accident and those days that followed are visceral feelings, as if I had suffered physical trauma. No words can capture the sadness. I was barely able to get out of bed or to get dressed. My patient family simply waited in the other room with their love at the ready if I needed it. I feel I must have gone temporarily deaf and mute.

Ian's death expedited my already planned move back to Minnesota for the start of medical school in September. To pass the time between packing and the funeral, my family and I lunched and brunched, walking down sidewalks past quaint Seattle coffee shops. The newsstands screamed bold headlines and front-page, grainy, black-and-white photos of Ian and the avalanche. Ian's face, larger than life, was everywhere I looked. The air was thick with the story of the Mount Baker avalanche. Relentless news on radio,

TV, and print rained down daily like broken glass on my soul. Ian looked handsome and fit.

Whatcom County Emergency Services provided volunteers and equipment to help in the search for Ian and Steve Raschick. Searchers are just a few of the thousands of volunteers in Washington State who form mountain rescue teams, with resources that include the German Shepherd Search Dogs and helicopters from the Whidbey Island Naval Air Station. One of the staff, Jan Leonardo, was described as speaking in a voice tattered with emotion and fatigue, that shows how the ripples in the wake of these accidents catch a wide array of people.

Then of course the debate that follows all accidents followed in subsequent articles. Talk of resources and risk; the whys and who should pay; the going over of details about the route and permits: should climbers have been there on that slope, on that day, at that exact time. "Is it worth the risk?"

The majority of questions addressed the risk and cost to society at large. It was a valid question, but so difficult for me just a few days after the accident while Ian's body rested deep in a crevasse.

It's estimated that all mountain climbers face a one in 1,750 chance of death from the sport. For those who venture above nineteen thousand feet (destinations such as Mount Everest) risk estimates climb to ten to twelve in one hundred. A number of other factors, such as route, time of year, and experience will affect the degree of risk. According to *Accidents in North American Mountaineering*, well known to many climbers, injuries peaked in North America at 210 in 1976. In 1986 there were 203 injuries with fewer than fifty deaths. That year we were young, with nothing to lose except our lives. The odds did not seem unreasonable given the reward of standing at the summit of one of the tallest peaks in the area.

"Is it worth the risk if you are the 'one'?" I still ask myself each time I venture into alpine terrain and when I recommend surgical procedures to my patients.

In the days after the avalanche, I went obsessively over and over that day, the route, the ropes, the weather, the could haves, the might haves, as if it were a complex mathematic problem to be solved, as if there were a possible solution to this impossibility, an alternative outcome. There was no math or reasoning that could change fate. I could not out-reason death. And yet I kept trying, endlessly ruminating about the details of that day.

Witness reports said that around 7:00 a.m., August 3, 1986, there was a noise and four climbers were seen, arms and legs flailing, sliding down the slope, all but one disappearing into the white void. The fourth, Tommy Waller, appeared to be tumbling on the top of the moving mass of ice and snow. Tommy was tossed across the crevasse by the force of the avalanche flow and ended up encased in snow in a sitting position, jammed onto his ice axe, ice block at his back, with broken ribs, a collapsed lung, and shoulder injuries. The crevasse that took the three others was a cavity eight to ten feet wide and fifty to seventy feet deep. Kurt Petellin was rescued from the crevasse by a party of climbers that included Steve Sieberson and Chris Moore, who were first on the scene. Kurt suffered a dislocated shoulder. While the rescuers were trying to follow the rope into the crevasse a second avalanche forced them to back off. A Canadian rescue team training in the area radioed for help.

Tommy said later he felt utterly erased, no pain, just blankness after the snow stopped moving. He described the silent mountain, blue sky, and blood colouring the snow around him.

"Jesus loves me. This I know because the Bible tells me so," he said to himself.

Within the first few days Kurt appeared on the *Today Show*, and the *National Enquirer* offered Tommy $2,500 for an interview which he declined. I visited Tommy in the hospital and talked to one of the rescuers, Harry Patz, who was involved in the search and rescue. All my research could not change the outcome, but I could not rest until I had all the details I could unearth.

Tommy sent me a letter the following fall:

Dearest Ellen,

...I was really joyfully surprised of the arrival of your letter...
I feel a lot of the same things you do, Ellen, and I hope you are
getting along well in Med School...The lord spared me and
Kurt, for what reason, is not evident at this time in my life.
I really thank the lord that you decided not to make the climb
also because I really think you are a special woman...
I still remember the day you came to see me in the hospital.
You really don't know how much that meant to me Ellen.
I knew that you cared and it warmed my heart...I don't know
if you have heard this poem before, but it really says a lot to
me and gives me the strength to go on living.

> *God hath not promised skies always blue,*
> *Flower strewn pathways all our lives through,*
> *God hath not promised sun without rain.*
> *Joy without sorrow, peace without pain.*
> *But God Hath promised strength for the day,*
> *Rest for the labour, light for the way.*
> *GRACE for the trails, help from above*
> *Unfailing sympathy, undying love.*

I hope this little message inspires you as it has me. May the
lord be with you Ellen. Have faith.

A giant — Mother Nature, Mount Baker, Fate, Random Chance? — had put her foot down. It was done. Hope was declared to be abandoned. Nothing to find. In spite of no body, the arrangements were made for a service.

On the day of Ian's funeral at a large Catholic church, a friend wore orange and yellow at my request to not wear depressing colours, while vultures (AKA the press) stalked us with their cameras at the entrance. I tried to find words, but my language confusion continued.

"I am so happy you came to our wedding, I mean funeral, oh I am sorry, I do mean funeral, so sorry..." I said to many people.

"Do not go gently into that good night," Ian's father read from the Dylan Thomas poem, "...though lovers be lost, love shall not."

The service included the psalm about walking through the shadow of death — familiar, but fitting and heartbreaking.

As a history major, Ian was deeply interested in the origins and stories of the Catholic Church, and religion in general; the bells and smells of the mass rituals delighted him. Although he did not necessarily agree with all the rules and regs, he would have approved of this traditional church service with friends and family. I do not believe he would have regretted climbing, just the aftermath of collective grief. His essence, I am sure, was there in the church impatiently urging us all to get out to the mountains.

"To the roundhouse, Mabel!" I could hear him saying.

After the service my family went back home, and between moving out of my apartment and heading back to Minnesota, I stayed with Ian's climbing partner Dave for a few days at his parents' formal, brick, colonial-style house facing a lush, well-manicured lawn in an older neighborhood in Seattle. One early sleepless morning, I was up wandering around the large hallways and rooms looking for the kitchen. I set off the alarm, waking his parents. I felt bad about the commotion. I was lost in unfamiliar surroundings. My life was dissolving like quicksand in all directions. I was no longer able to locate the kitchen, my toothbrush, or the bathroom, not to mention my lover.

The "in-between" after Ian's death was populated by an extended group of friends, family, and strangers who offered kind words, hugs, and gentle hands on my arm. Help in those days and weeks came at the moments I most needed it. This communal enveloping support was offered to me when I was unable to catalogue all that was given in time, tasks, and words. A cozy fog surrounded me without face or form. Everyone was there for me, although it's hard to remember all the details. Time stopped and compressed and expanded until it ceased to exist, and then became a single moment in my mind and in my memory.

The week I was scheduled to leave Washington State my older brother Patrick flew into Seattle to drive back with me in Murray. Patrick is number three of the seven siblings, the only left-hander, quieter than the rest of us, always deeply helpful, and well known to all his family for practical skills like fixing cars. Since the chance of breaking down on a cross-country road trip is inversely proportional to the size of your toolbox, Patrick arrived with a very large toolbox. Murray, the peeling, yellow, racing stripe decals looking shabbier than ever, gave us no trouble on the journey back to Minnesota.

My rational mind tells me that we must have driven during the day, but my memories of that long trek across the northwestern United States are only of dark nights with faintly lit highways, mostly empty, and infrequent truck stops along the apparently nocturnal route. We traveled 1,624 miles to Minnesota. We arrived at the looming, old, gray, wood-sided Victorian house that Patrick and his wife Suzy had just purchased in the small town of Stillwater. I will swear it was during a thunderstorm and that the house was haunted. A truly dark and stormy night punctuated by thunder and lightning welcomed me home.

PART III

EMBRYOLOGY
origins of a finished product

MY DOG PAL LOUP (RIP) WAS MY DEAR COMPANION
FOR MANY YEARS.

fig. 3–1

RUDIMENTS

---

starting from scratch

In September, 1986, it rained cadavers. Medical school started that month with human dissections in gross anatomy. It was only weeks after the avalanche, and grief encased me like molasses; my subconscious desperately ran around inside me, poking and prodding, prying me forward from minute to minute, pushing like a miniscule Sisyphus to keep me from sliding down into the darkness. From above, my family and friends were pulling for me, encouraging and generous. My rational mind appreciated the support, but my emotional mind still longed to disappear into eternity.

Here is where grief introduced herself. What came before was shock and emptiness. The day of and the in between was not grieving. Those early days were focused on whether I could stand or speak, struggling to even believe that Ian was gone.

Grief, like the wind, is a concrete and powerful entity that you cannot see, cannot catch in your hand to hold, cannot hold out to others to show them what you feel. My grief was a shadow, a ghost, lurking just underneath what looked like an ordinary life. Like wind-scattered fragments of autumn leaves I was buffeted between moments of sobbing and staring off into space. Every once in a while a laugh or a small joy would lift me, but grief was always there to pull me back to sorrow.

Every time I looked in the mirror, I was surprised. Who was this fit, toned, tanned, young woman who had recently been climbing mountains? I half expected to see an ancient sea witch with crazy white hair and deep wrinkles like crevasses around hollowed eyes. My bed would not swallow me up no matter how long I lay there, nor would the earth or sand. I could not escape Grief. I carried a mental image of myself seated in a rocking chair, covered with a shawl or blanket, staring into space, with no connection to or awareness of reality reflected in my eyes, which were vacant, empty, free. At the same time, my descent into mourning felt impossibly self-centred, the opposite of the healing caregiver I was supposedly training to become.

Right after Ian's death, I had called the medical school to see if I could delay my start.

"Unfortunately, the medical school is unable to offer anything other than an immediate start or a full one-year deferment," the tough administrator, who was also a psychologist, declared. That was it. Jump in or wait a full year. Waiting a year felt like a death sentence. It seemed that if I did not keep going and put one foot in front of the other, I would lie down and never get up again. So I jumped in. Facing the biggest mountain of my life so far, I stepped forward and started school as planned. Step. Rest. Step. Rest. Repeat. Repeat. Repeat.

First term in medical school includes gross anatomy, gross in the sense of general, not disgusting. Anatomy is part of the first classes because it forms the basis, gives the rudiments, of medical training. The anatomy lab was on the upper floor of an old building that reminded me of my 1960s elementary school. It smelled like the old white paste that our first-grade teacher dished out to us from a tall, plastic jar with a wooden spatula to spread on our primary colour, construction paper projects — the paste that we grade schoolers always wanted to eat. The cadaver lab was a large rectangular room – two old classrooms with the wall removed; big windows lined the exterior walls; natural light streamed into the space like an alternative heaven.

Cadavers filled the room, intact bodies cast in the opaque beige of embalming fixative, all oriented the same direction, like a school of fish swimming upstream. These inert bodies were stiff and colourless, reminiscent of the Mexican Sierra fish Steinbeck describes in his *Log from the Sea of Cortez*. These embalmed citizens were catalogued in exactly the same way as those lifeless fish, in contrast to a live fish on a line with colours pulsing, or the breathing humans casting their lines. Our cadaver specimens reclined supine on stainless steel tables as if napping, their former lives hidden behind fixed flesh. Teams of four students per body counted bones and pickled organs, cataloguing the husks of lives once lived.

Each donated body was different due to age, size, gender, prior injuries or surgeries. From day to day, teams shared interesting findings.

"Hey, check this out," a fellow student exclaimed one day.

We crowded around his cadaver to see an enormous hernia. In the early part of the twentieth century, large hernias were managed with special trusses or garments to push the hernia back into place, to avoid a dangerous surgery; from the size of it, this man likely lived with his hernia for many years. Before techniques were advanced enough to make the surgical correction of hernias safe, early editions of *Gray's Anatomy* had a whole section dedicated to the paraphernalia used to hold in the hernia.

Another time teams were using mallets and chisels to try to dissect the inner ear without smashing it.

"I got it," a student yelled.

"Wow!"

"That's amazing."

"I can't believe you didn't damage the stapes."

We took turns leaning in to see the beautiful inner ear dissection, the miniscule stapes bone intact. I silently thanked all the bodies for their generous spirit of giving, then often slipped out of the cadaver lab into the hall to stifle tears. That hallway was lined with standard, mid-century, stained maple doors, light gold, and flecked terrazzo floor, a shade of olive-gray smoothly narrowing in perspective, disappearing at the end of the long corridor. The flat cold floor was oddly comforting, its ancient patina a record of the footsteps of decades of students who had preceded me. The sheer timelessness of this old building gave me strength. The stone stairs were worn down in the middle from the combined weight of all who had ever climbed them. These traces of former students encouraged me to keep following the path forward.

My anatomy professor Doctor Parsons began to notice when I slipped out, and would join me in the hall for a few minutes, waiting patiently and silently while I collected myself sufficiently to return to class. There were many days that I wept, silently trying desperately not to weep, Doctor Parsons beside me, quiet, a kindred spirit. He had wisdom born from tragedy, and could comfort with a few soft words or unspoken support. Immensely kind and calm, he stood solidly beside me in the old empty hallway outside the gross anatomy lab for as long as it took. He was like an oak tree that had weathered many storms and remained to provide shelter from rain and wind. He had learned the lessons grief has to teach, and in his calm way he taught me much more than gross anatomy. He seemed to know that Grief cannot be rushed.

Cadavers are preserved with formaldehyde, and, in spite of gloves, the smell of that strong chemical permeates fingers and hands. That evil smell followed me out of the lab and was with me for the rest of each day; that damned smell persisted no matter how many times I washed my hands. During those autumn months, every time I tried to eat and my hands came too close to my face I would smell formaldehyde. Like Proust's petite madeleine, which smell brought the town of Combray to life, the scent of formaldehyde summoned images of dead bodies to rise up from my plate every day at dinner.

Each medical student was issued a human skull in a wooden case as part of gross anatomy. The blonde case was about eight inches square and eleven inches tall, with a handle on the top. We were expected to take our skulls home to study in the evenings after classes, and on the bus back and forth to school, I would clutch my skull-in-a-box on my lap, worried at every sudden stop or bump that the box would fall to the floor and the skull would escape to roll down the aisle. The city bus passengers were a quilt-work of citizens: students, the elderly, mothers with children, and those who smelled of homelessness who did not seem likely to have enough change to even ride the bus — did the drivers take pity and let them on without fare? These long, tall buses with their old plastic seats and large windows lurched around corners and staggered across uneven pavement, the sagging pull-cords swaying like a conductor's baton orchestrating the scene.

I imagined the bus hitting a deep pothole, rocking violently, and me dropping the wooden box, the top flying open, and the skull making its getaway. My skull would roll unevenly down the aisle with a soft irregular thumping for one or two revolutions before tipping to settle on that flat part of the temple or the bottom of the mandible. Children shrieking, horrified passengers wide-eyed, whites showing like terrified horses. How does one explain a skull-in-a-box? I told myself the box was a carefully constructed, wooden vessel with sturdy brass clips to hold it closed, and I clutched it tightly on my lap at all times.

My skull in its special wood box became a friend. The rich pine box with shiny brass hardware protected the smooth, off-white, contoured bones that gave away no secrets. Skull was always there, always the same, waiting quietly for the next outing, a perfect pal, quiet and constant. Death had come and gone, yet the skull was in pristine condition, ready and willing to teach hidden gems that build the landscape of our faces. Who was this person before meeting me as a skull? Years later I met an old surgeon at the Harvard Medical Writers Conference, who was a few decades ahead of me in his career. He confessed to having had a warm feeling about the skull he had studied years before.

"We called him Archibald," the white-haired surgeon told me with a wrinkled smile, both of us pleased to share this strange experience of having a skull-in-a-box as a teaching companion.

At school it became clear that the line between life and death in my world had truly and suddenly been erased. Life and death were fluid, nothing seemed real. Skulls and cadavers were people, each with a story, most with loved ones left behind. Unbearably sad. And at the same time it was so fascinating and so fabulous that all these dead people had given us the gift of their bodies to study, their preserved bodies obscuring the reality of who they had been. If those people, now called cadavers, who donated their bodies, could have awakened for a moment to tell their stories, I feel sure it would have made me feel better. It would have been more instructive than the lessons their bones and organs taught. How much can you learn about a person from just their bodies? They could have told me the path forward and how to take the best lessons from a hard time. After all, they must have been good and generous people to end up in the gross anatomy lab, teaching even after death.

I used all the energy I could muster to cultivate a calm exterior to get through each day. I felt the bottomless pit of shadows lurking under the old concrete floors, a dark bog poised to drag me down at any moment. Grief was a formidable opponent. The gravity of Grief shadowed me like a personal ghost, one only I could see.

"You are okay," I told my reflection in the mirror almost every time I went into the bathroom, whether at home or at school, as if saying it out loud would make it true.

I continued to be amazed that there was no physical mark on me. I felt my skin should be peeling off, or I should break out in weeping rashes or be covered in bruises. I should look like an old spook from a 1960s zombie movie, with a decayed arm or minus one leg. Instead, I looked fit and slimmer than usual due to weight loss from stress (even in the midst of this, I noticed my gaunt looks made me more like a supermodel). The only clue to my turmoil was the fact I wore the same electric blue shorts, a large white "Big Dog" logo emblazoned on the seat, every day for the first two months of medical school.

"What name should I take now that I am no longer Ellen?" I asked my reflection, who did not answer.

Once, during that first term in medical school, I went to the walk-in clinic in a moment of despair. The young provider, whose credentials I don't recall, offered to give me pills on the spot, clearly overwhelmed by my grief.

"I'm sorry," I found myself apologizing to her, "I don't need a prescription, I just was looking for other suggestions."

She shifted slightly in her chair and put her hands on the desk and then back in her lap, at a loss for words. Clearly, I was making her uncomfortable, so I quickly left without pills or advice to carry on as best I could. Barely able to care for myself, I could not help her deal with my pain. Step. Rest. Step. Rest. Repeat. Repeat. Repeat.

Since then I have seen many therapists — some helpful and some not. One always sat on a five-wheeled office chair and would zoom up really close to make a point before rolling back to her listening distance. Another mostly nodded, but never smiled, although she did tell me that touch and smell are helpful to calm your amygdala, otherwise known as your oldest lizard brain; that turned out to be good advice. I'll still dab lavender or peppermint oil on my skin, or light a scented candle, and relish petting my dog or carrying a smooth stone in my pocket. After she told me that, I instantly understood why Captain Queeg in the 1954 movie *The Caine Mutiny* always rolled those two steel balls around in his hand.

Since there was no severe physical injury or scar to mark the pain of Ian's death, I longed for a scarlet letter, a big black letter "D" to show how injured I was. Perhaps that's why I wore the Big Dog shorts. How could people not see that my appearance as a young, successful, first-year medical student was a hologram, a fiction?

"My boyfriend just died," I introduced myself to everyone I met.

This might put most people off, but my student colleagues, often with challenges themselves (including two wheelchair-bound due to spinal injuries), just went with it. They were all willing to go out of their way for me. Several colleagues were on their second careers, having been engineers or allied health professionals. A few had children or were single parents, and at least one got pregnant that first year. All were accepting.

Having nothing to lose was an invitation to do things I might not do now. For about a year I had no fear of death. I even tempted death, taking revenge on fate by dangling my own life in front of the Reaper's nose.

"Bring it, world," was my mindset. "I dare you, Reaper!"

I dabbled in ice climbing, fun but more technical and less creative than rock climbing. Ice climbing is more dangerous because the ice is always changing, potentially too soft, with no handholds, or too brittle, shattering like glass. Recklessness is intoxicating. Ice climbing on a frozen waterfall in a quarry in St. Paul, Minnesota, I rationalized the risk as being similar to the chance of getting hit by a car, which actually seemed more likely. I was so distracted by my internal struggle there was a real possibility I might cross the street in front of a bus in my fog of ruminations. Ice climbing was safer for me because I was focused. When not focused I was lost. What I didn't understand yet, was that I would have to pick myself up and start from scratch.

My mind reflected back repeatedly to the pre-death days. My birthday in June, when Ian had rented the sea kayaks and introduced me to the ocean, he'd said it was a different beast then freshwater, with different dangers and different gifts. To my freshwater eyes, with years of experience in rivers and streams, the sea seemed to hide ghouls — it still does, like those in a childhood closet, the ones you don't recognize until it is too late. But the ocean also has a bounty of joys, and that trip we were offered any number of fabulous surprises by the daily tides, including starfish and seals, and the bioluminescent waves.

"This is the best year of my life," I said one time to a fellow medical student in the fall of 1986.

We looked at each other in stunned silence for a second — the student was well aware of my backstory — and then I started to laugh. I had finally found my words, but lost my filters, blurting out whatever thoughts were top of mind, discarding all the usual social norms of casual interactions.

"Hey, what's new," a former high school classmate asked me on fall break at our hometown bar, Brookside, in Marine on Saint Croix.

"My boyfriend died, and I'm dissecting cadavers in my gross anatomy class."

I have no idea how that brash announcement was really received, but I don't recall her being as distressed as the young psychologist at the walk-in clinic. Perhaps I was developing a rapid assessment of others to gauge their ability to handle my grief — throw my loss in their faces and if they recoil in horror, move on; if not, they might be friend material.

The past clawed at the present. Images of our apartment in Seattle, that second-floor unit near Lake Union, the living room with our neat piles of gear, the patterned oriental rug, all vied for attention with the tasks at hand. For months after he died, I wore Ian's running shoes, looking down at my feet, seeing his. Driving in

Minneapolis, I'd suddenly think I was in Seattle. Not recognizing the streets or intersections, I would have to pull over to wrestle my attention back to the present day, to try to orient myself to the new surroundings. I suffered from more and more nightmares, waking up standing by the side of the bed. A sleepwalker and intense dreamer my whole life, this was not unexpected, but still distressing. I woke up more than once seeing Ian standing outside the window on a little ledge. Other nights I would be at base camp, knowing he would die, but letting him go nevertheless.

In one recurring dream, I called Ian over and over on the telephone, listening to endless rings on a static-filled line. Later I learned of a "wind phone" in a garden on a hilltop in Japan. The phone was in a white metal and glass telephone booth, both created by Itaru Sasaki, a seventy-year-old gardener, so he could speak to his lost cousin. The "wind phone" overlooks Otsuchi town and the Pacific Ocean. Thousands of people found solace there in the wake of the devastating 2011 tsunami, and it became a way to keep in contact with the dead and missing. Imagine voices traveling across the wind to lost loved ones. My nightly dream calls were my own wind phone.

Once I dreamed there was evil in the house eating holes like a moth in everything, decaying all in its path. Regardless of the night traumas, every day I rode the bus to school, with my skull-in-a-box clutched on my lap, on my way to face a roomful of cadavers. During the day there were times that I reached for the phone to call Ian, only to remind myself he was dead. It was easier to imagine he had simply stayed behind in Seattle than to picture his body in that crevasse. Cadavers and skulls surrounding me, I was haunted by Ian for those weeks at the start of medical school.

He was still buried in the snow and ice. Dead but not gone.

CLASSIC STUDY POSE. EVEN TO THIS DAY I CAN BE FOUND IN THIS POSE
ONCE IN A WHILE WITH A LAPTOP KEYBOARD IN PLACE OF PEN AND PAPER.

fig. 3–2

CHRONOLOGICAL TABLES

_____

strict schedules wait for no one

Just like the predictable forty weeks of fetal development, medical school follows a strict four-year schedule that cannot be altered (even if someone dies). In the fall of 1986, in addition to gross anatomy, I attended daily basic science lectures, which were to continue for two years. Every day all two hundred or so students would file into the large auditorium the size of a smallish movie theater, with flip-down, worn, upholstered seats, each with a small, fold-out, Formica desktop. The lecture hall could have been lifted from the 1973 movie *The Paper Chase,* except instead of Harvard Law School, this was medical school at the University of Minnesota.

And now there were a few more women, though classes were still predominantly male. We faced a podium in front of a large screen. Professors who seemed to be speaking high-speed gibberish, raced through a slide per minute, each slide a full page of text, for the entire lecture. Even had I known shorthand, or was not preoccupied with my personal tragedy, the volume of facts was so large there was no way to record it during the lecture. I once tried to sit in the front row and take notes at an early morning lecture, but instead fell asleep halfway through.

I had been warned that taking in the amount of information presented in the first year of medical school would be like trying to take a drink from a fire hose. That was not an exaggeration. There were no personal computers or internet, so the students formed a note co-op where one student per class gathered the slides and handouts for every lecture, making a hundred or more photocopies of the material at the local copy shop for distribution to co-op members. Each lecture resulted in several pages of variable quality, black-and-white photocopies to study along with the textbook chapters assigned for review. Between textbooks and lecture notes, we were buried in paper.

I would sit at my kitchen table or at a desk in the library for hours to read pages in rapid succession, committing all to short-term memory. I've always had a good memory, and it was in overdrive during these years. Some of my classmates were not so lucky, having to study each page multiple times, a Herculean task given the massive number of pages required to study before each test. In hindsight, which is my only tool to recollect (and I can almost hear Ian getting ready to debate this with me), it is possible that grief was helping me out by cocooning me like a tightly swaddled baby.

I was so very drawn into myself that I was not easily distracted or particularly interested in anything else at all. It made no difference to me if I was studying for several hours straight or staring off into space; it all felt the same. I had nothing better to do than sit in the same chair for hours on end. Actually, I did have a real interest in the subjects, so these long study sessions gave me a break from Mistress Grief—she seemed to step back as if respecting my need to concentrate on my studies. That said, most of the time she was a terrible taskmaster, constantly pulling me down, pulling me back, heavier than our giant backpacks with fresh food and wine, and to carry her was more tiring than climbing any mountain. So studying and being expected to learn an almost unlearnable amount of material in a finite amount of time turned out to be a welcome break from Mistress Grief cracking her own musty whip.

During exam week, clusters of students would gather in the commons outside the lecture hall on the hideous, light-and-dark-orange, worn-out, seventies-style, Naugahyde lounge chairs to review and compare notes. Students challenged one another for hours in the library with hundreds of flash cards made from three-by-five-inch, ruled index cards, each with a notation or formula on one side and a single word in large letters on the flip side. I remember a tiny Krebs Cycle diagram, the basic formula for energy derived from carbohydrates, fat, and proteins, the formula written so small it was hardly legible.

"Cranial nerves," my study partner would announce while holding up a card.

"On Old Olympus' Towering Top A Fin And German Viewed Some Hops," I would say.

"And?" my partner would insist.

"Okay." I would take a breath. "The first O, cranial nerve one, olfactory, which is key to smell; number two, old, optic nerve the largest nerve in the body; Olympus is number three, the oculomotor nerve that serves the eyelid and eye movements; number four the "Towering" trochlear nerve that serves again the eye movements and is exceptionally susceptible to trauma. Trigeminal is next that serves facial sensation; then Abducens number six that is a common source of double vision as it serves the lateral eye muscles; and then the facial which is the "Fin" the seventh, that is responsible for Bell's palsy and serves the facial muscles; the eight, that is the auditory; then the glossopharygial, the vagus, and the hypoglossal—the twelve cranial nerves."

This and other mnemonics and sayings stick in my mind from those years of hammering them in.

"You are not dead until you are cold and dead." Which is to say hypothermia victims might appear to be dead but sometimes can be revived, which weirdly now appears to apply to cell phone batteries—not dead until warm and dead.

"Better is the enemy of good." A useful saying for both surgeons and artists; generally a way to say, stop whatever you are doing while the outcome still looks pretty good, because if you keep working on it then it will just get worse and worse.

"First of all, take your own pulse." Great advice to health care providers as a way not to panic. Panic is not conducive to good choices. And so many more medical clichés that carry a lot more than an ounce of truth.

During the weeks leading up to exams my visual memory became so sticky that whatever I looked at stuck, including advertisements or a tabloid headline at the supermarket check-out, like "Woman with the World's Smallest Face!" My ability to see things and store them in my brain was an asset for exams, but also helped a boy in a skeleton suit run into my dreams, and is why I still cannot watch horror movies.

Dreams are a big sorting task, where the brain is trying to archive everything you saw in the day in order to reset for the coming day. A lot like Ian and I lining up all our gear on the living room floor between each trip. I remember vividly a dream I had about a year after Ian's death. I was in an ambulance, driving backwards down a road at an impossibly fast rate of speed, about fifty miles per hour, being chased by a running child in a skeleton suit who was able to keep up at highway speeds. I knew, even in my sleep, the ambulance had driven into my psyche via my seeing them daily at the hospital, but what the heck was the kid in the skeleton suit doing there? Was I, in fact, losing my mind, the part that was not already lost to grief?

I puzzled about the skeleton suit boy for a few weeks, until at a friend's house, standing in front of her refrigerator, there he was—her five-year-old son, dressed in a skeleton suit for Halloween, smiling back at me from the array of photos taped to the front of the refrigerator. I was relieved. The skeleton suit boy had run into my dreams from my friend's refrigerator door. Decades later, I can still pull up memories like the walkway outside the medical school, made of textured concrete with slender gray concrete vines curving in between pebbles protruding from the smooth cement, just enough to give a person purchase in the winter frost to avoid a slip and fall.

My brain was so full I was in danger of forgetting my own name. I could feel my cerebral cortex buzzing with electricity. Like the shelves of an old-fashioned, wooden pantry, my brain was stacked high with rows of facts, like the canning bounty of a bumper crop of delicious red tomatoes, with no more room to store all the new knowledge. Hundreds of histology slides, every bone in the human body, the Krebs cycle, all the biochemistry needed to keep a body alive each hour and every day vied for space, eventually pushing other canning jar facts to the edge of the pantry shelf to fall off and roll away, facts like where the car keys ended up at the end of the day.

Going to medical school was a lot like going back to kindergarten. Just as five-year-olds follow their teacher to the lunchroom or out for recess, our more adult class formed a giant amoeba of students moving en masse from lecture hall to lab and back.

We had a pathology professor who looked like a perfect kindergarten teacher, with her endless wardrobe of nearly identical cotton dresses, all in various plain navy blue to plaid brown tones with proper white curved collars, sometimes with buttons on the front, her hair always exactly the same. She must have been June Cleaver's mother's twin—June was the quintessential 1950s housewife from the television show *Leave It to Beaver*. Just looking at her reminded me of grade school in the 1960s. I half expected her to pull out the white jars of paste with the popsicle sticks to spread it around—which reminded me now of tongue depressors. I wonder if she wore a wig—she was that perfect. She spoke in firm and measured words with soft authority that precluded argument, as if she had been born a fully clothed professor in those old academic halls on the first day the doors opened for students. This professor, with her old-fashioned fashion, was a maverick in her understated way.

After all, what percentage of pathology professors had been female in medical schools at the time she had trained?

To add to my feeling that I had gone back to grade school, I had an odd encounter on one of my first days.

"Did you carry a Mickey Mouse school bus lunch box in grade school?" My fellow classmate, a tall red-headed, fair skinned, freckled young man asked me.

"Yes, I did," I replied.

He pointed to his front tooth, then went on to remind me that I had accidently hit him in the mouth and chipped his tooth all those years ago in grade school while joyfully swinging my favorite metal lunch box. I recalled the box, which was rectangular, on the top a bright orange school bus design showing Disney characters, including Mickey Mouse cheerfully looking out the painted windows. Weird that we had gone to the same grade school, and he should remember me because I hit him in the mouth with a metal box. I remembered the lunch box and my classmate, but not the teeth smashing.

In the small spaces of time between days of labs, lectures and exams, we had parties and danced, as if trying to shake off all of our newly gained knowledge, under the acoustic blanket of Bananarama's "I'm Your Venus". My classmate Eric, a late twentieth-century Fred Astaire on the dance floor, could finesse a perfect performance from any willing dance partner including me. Brad had a wild vibe. He would stand to my side like a tumbling coach, hands at my back and hip, and count "one, two, three", at which point I would jump up in the middle of the party crowd for him to flip me into an aerial somersault, feet over head, to land on my feet again without missing a beat, and without kicking any of the other gyrating nerds in the face on the way down.

These first months of medical school were the end and the beginning, exciting and awful, the hardest academic and emotional term of my life so far, a crucible of despair and learning.

I still wrote letters to Ian in the form of a journal. As I wrote I'd return to the alpine slopes dotted with wildflowers in the August sun, snow-covered peaks sparkling above. Ian would join me in the meadows.

"This is so much more complicated than sadness or anger."

Ian smiles, his blue eyes kind. "Tell me more."

"I don't know," I reply. We walk together in silence side by side, looking out over the wild beauty.

After a while I say, "It's everything really, all rolled up into an impossible tangle. There is grief and sorrow and shock and disbelief. Melancholy, loneliness, anger, frustration, hopelessness, paralysis, desperation, fear, and emptiness — I guess it's insanity."

Ian puts his hand to his mouth to blow me a kiss. I understand he can no longer physically comfort me. Tears streak my face.

"I feel like going to a public place, a street corner or city park, to shriek and wail — to throw all these feelings away into the rest of humanity's pool of pain and suffering."

"I know," he says simply.

I feel him there on that grassy slope and the clean mountain air and hear the gentle wind.

"I wish I could stay here forever with you," I say. "I am too pitiful and self-centred to be of any use to anyone in the real world."

He just smiles. "You and I both know that isn't true. It's perfectly okay to be broken. If you can't see the wound, then you can't heal. You know that, Ellen. I know you do."

But I could not stay forever in that mountain meadow. I had to face reality each morning. I had to get dressed and carry my skull-in-a-box to all the cadavers, and try to look like all the other medical students. I was a med student by day, fighting off grief at the end of every day. She was giving me a solid daily beating, and what I did not know yet is that I should not have been fighting her so hard. Grief was not going to let me go until I faced her. I would drift back to my alpine slope where I began to shiver, feeling the coldness of the crevasse, when I could no longer exist in the real world.

"How am I going to ever get over your death?"

"Come on, let's walk," Ian says.

We walk to the edge of the meadow and sit on top of a cliff that plummets down to one of the glaciers winding its way down the mountain. Our feet dangle over the edge. I feel the warm sun on my face and the cool air coming off the ice below.

"Maybe I should jump off. That way I could be with you forever."

"You could. But you shouldn't. I'm not sure it works like that."

"Don't you know how it works now that you've left? What's it like?"

"I'm not sure yet," Ian says slowly. "It's not bad, though."

"Life is so stupid. Why bother living when all we're doing is marching towards death. Why am I even alive anymore? I should have gone on that climb with you. We're just a bunch of dumb mammals having babies so that they can die too. Honestly, what's even the point of living?"

Ian tilts his head, smiling again. "You'll be okay. I know you will."

"I can't even sleep because I'm having too many nightmares. I don't think I can do this."

"You can. I'm here for you. Remember the rest step? You can climb this mountain."

In a way I was lazy, letting the strict structure and schedules of medical school carry me forward. I got up each morning, got dressed, faced my skull and cadavers, and pretended that everything was okay. And then I took myself to task in my journal.

I am so pitiful in my self-centredness.

I wish to cast off this chill of death which enveloped my soul upon Ian's death, to throw it from me violently and run in desperation towards life. At the same moment I want to abandon myself to death, to embrace death, to end this foolishness called life which could be more aptly named "the vigil awaiting death" — what is life but the denial of death? What are we but senseless creations of molecules senselessly procreating to achieve an unsatisfactory immortality, pretending all along that procreation is not the main goal in life. Ian. My soulmate. A troubled man, a questioning man. My link to life. He is dead. Why am I still alive? How can one live with this inevitable end?

If I thought I could recapture the communion I had with Ian by dying I would commit suicide. I am at the edge of life; where Ian had stood there is an incomprehensible void. I do not understand. I look with blind eyes, and I look always towards this void. Perhaps tomorrow I will write about Ian's death. For now I'll sleep — no doubt have nightmares. I search for understanding even in my sleep.

That was if I could sleep at all.

MY MOM, KATHERINE ANDERSON, PICTURED HERE PICKING ME
UP AFTER THE FORTY-TWO DAY KAZAN RIVER CANOE TRIP.

fig. 3 – 3

MATURATION

"the child is the father of the man" — *Wordsworth*

Soon after I arrived back in Minnesota, on that truly dark and stormy night, I recognized that I must seek backwards to move forward. Ian I'm sure would agree that historical inquiry has the power to inform the present, although I hold the "problem of hindsight" in my mind. I knew my most recent past, my time with Ian, held no promise — at least not for my immediate future. And there was no present scaffold for the future, except for the medical school curriculum that marched ahead with cruel neutrality.

Just a year earlier, with the typical sass and bravado of youth, I had left to explore the world, never dreaming I would be coming home a year later with the wind knocked out of me, confused by circumstances. I struggled to get my bearings, trying to remember the time before part of me went missing, sifting through memories scattered across my mind like old Polaroids, fading with age. I was lost in what had been familiar surroundings. Lost in myself.

By the time the trees were showing off their fall colours, the me I had been was buried under the turbulent rubble of death and the avalanche of cadavers, with grief dogging me every step of the way. In spite of my fog of emotion and a barrage of unending medical facts, I knew there was a kernel somewhere, a part of me that was not fully destroyed, that could be an anchor, a starting point for the road back up. First, I had to find her.

As number six of seven kids in a chaotic, but loving family, I always felt part of something bigger than me. I was always aware that I am just a thread in the larger fabric, no less important and no more important than any other thread. As in a climbing rope, all the strands are needed. The seven of us were free every summer to run wild in bare feet with our friends in the neighborhood. The nooks and secret paths through small spaces, between hedges and backyard fences were well worn by the packs of kids, including ours. The soles of our bare feet were black with dirt by dusk. The worst thing that might happen in a day was to step in dog poo, the disgusting, slimy, brown mess pushing between bare toes. Avoiding the piles was a challenge as we raced around the neighborhood labyrinth of trails.

Around age six, my young friends and I discovered a tree in one of our backyards, with a curled-in section up the middle that made it look like buttocks, which of course we named "The Butt Tree," where we met to tell one another secrets. In our childish minds it was a sacred place, the location not to be shared with anyone outside our group. In retrospect, this tree in the backyard of my friend's house was a grade-school version of the wind phone, the secluded place we went to talk, to let loose our secrets into the world. In the quiet of summer, snuggled into the greenery of the surrounding bushes, it was a perfect hide-out to get away from adults and older siblings.

Our street, Osceola Avenue in St. Paul, still had lumpy gray and umber cobblestone pavement from a century ago, one of the only cobblestone streets in the city. This unique feature made those of us who lived there feel part of a special group. More than sixty children thrived on that single city block. As long as we were home by six o'clock for dinner, followed by a soak in the tub to rinse off the day's adventures and the caked-on dirt from our bare feet, life was good. Perhaps it was that era, or maybe because there were so many children in our household, but my parents did not feel the need to keep a close watch on us. Kids and parents all knew we looked out for one another; we were free to traipse up and down our street; we had few obligations: nightly dinner always at six o'clock, washing dishes, Saturday chores, Sunday church, and of course school.

When we got older we had our bikes with banana seats and sissy bars. My banana seat was a fantastic, sparkly, neon-pink plastic. I also delighted in collecting bugs from under the smooth, flat stones in the side garden, dumping them from a paper Dixie cup onto the kitchen floor, the smooth vinyl perfect for viewing the potato bugs with their brownish-gray ridged backs and with what looked like hundreds of legs. The oval bugs curved into tiny balls if tipped on their backs. Sometimes I used clear tape to trap them on the linoleum for a bit before releasing them back into the side garden.

We seven children grew up in a four-bedroom, one bathroom, early twentieth-century, white stucco house with black trim; we had dogs, guinea pigs, and later a lizard that my sister named Ziggy Stardust, and a chinchilla with soft, gray fur.

My mother, who was always adventurous, bought us a cow's eye to dissect when I was about seven. She opened the package, surrounded by all the siblings, aged five to teens. All seven of us crowded around the table and leaned in to get a better look. The eye was squishy on the white butcher paper with the coloured iris down. Then all of us shrieked as my mother flipped the cow eye over so it was looking up at us with its liquid brown iris. A lot like the inner ear dissection in the cadaver lab, minus the shrieking.

"You have the world by the tail on a downhill slope," my father always told me. It was a powerful image, me taking the world wherever I wanted — at the same time feeling that the world might run me over.

Intrepid local travelers, my parents took their pack of offspring camping in the tall pine forests of northern Minnesota almost every year. My first camping trip was as an infant, six weeks old. One year, the nine of us piled into a classic station wagon with a pop-up trailer in tow for a drive all the way to the East Coast. For me as a grade schooler it was a fantastic adventure. I was small enough to enjoy the flip-up seats in the way-way back of the station wagon. I'm guessing my older brothers and sisters do not remember it as fondly, their larger bodies crushed into the back seats in the jumble of younger brothers and sisters, one brother car sick almost every trip. We may not share the same version of our collective childhood, but most of us still share a level of solidarity, exactly why it was natural that the majority of my siblings showed up in Seattle after the accident, because that's what we do — we show up.

Returning from that three-week, 1960s road trip, we trundled down the cobblestones of Osceola Avenue, pop-up trailer bumping behind and windows rolled down. All the neighborhood kids gathered to run along the sidewalks down the hill to welcome us home.

My favorite toys were wooden blocks cut from two-by-fours, Lincoln Logs, and canned goods from the cupboards that were good for stacking, and making imaginary cities; these were the canned goods that returned to fill up my brain that first term of medical school — imagine cans of basic medical science facts in place of Campbell's Soup. We played in the sunroom of our Osceola Avenue house, light through all the old windows shining down, filtered light flowing in just like in the cadaver lab, the old casements in the lab just a larger version of those in the sunroom.

My sister Meg is closest to me in age, number five of seven, and we had matching baby dolls with plastic limbs sewn onto cloth bodies, pink plastic heads with swirly, acrylic blond hair needle-pointed onto the plastic scalp giving them an air of having just awakened. The twin dolls shared a perpetually slight smile, detailed eyes with drawn-on lashes that opened upon sitting up, perfectly painted hazel irises aligned in a life-like stare, and each would squeak when you squeezed their bodies. Early on I gave my doll a squeaker-ectomy with a cut from neck to belly, closing her up with large loose hand stitches, so I always knew which doll was mine. The scar looked like a child's version of a sternotomy for open heart surgery.

My doll still sits looking slightly spooky in the dark recesses of my closet next to all those other archival items, her detailed irises and perfectly aligned pupils unchanged over the years. I also have my gray and black donkey Stuffy from that era. I pulled off his ear once in a tantrum, and he has one eye glued back in place, giving him a quizzical expression.

Along with my fascination with bugs, investigating doll squeakers, and repairing stuffed animals, I was determined, even as a small child, to become a doctor. There were no physicians in my immediate family, just distant uncles practicing medicine in Wisconsin, who my Grandma Mary always spoke of proudly. I do not recall parental pressure, just an idea encoded in my genes, or perhaps the so-called pressure was all encompassing or so subtle that I did not recognize it as such. If I'd gone into the church like Jenny, perhaps I would say it was a calling, but a calling from whom?

Every Sunday night we watched *Mutual of Omaha's Wild Kingdom* with Jim Fowler and Marlin Perkins and the *Wonderful World of Disney* on our tiny, black-and-white, twelve-inch screen. We watched every new episode of *Star Trek* featuring the youthful Leonard Nimoy and William Shatner, who finally went to the edge of space in 2021. This was a favorite, along with Mel Brooks' *Get Smart*, featuring Don Adams as the bumbling Agent 86, Maxwell Smart who, among other things, talked on a shoe phone, foreshadowing cell phones.

Neil Armstrong's first step on the moon, the picture of Phan Thi Kim Phuc, whom I only knew as the napalm girl at the time, and my first-grade teacher's husband going MIA in Vietnam were the backdrop to "See Spot Run". My oldest brother Mark was required to register for the draft during the Vietnam War; although he was never called up, the family watched the mail for a notice with daily anxiety in anticipation that the violent world portrayed on our tiny television would reach in to capture our own flesh and blood. Mark marched on that same small, black-and-white screen, performing with the Michigan State University band for President Richard Nixon's inauguration in 1973. Ian and I had much of this history in common, albeit from different geographic perspectives.

Fears of nuclear war, carried over from the Cuban Missile Crisis of 1962, presented the real threat to a young child watching the ambient news, that a nuclear attack could be imminent. There was a bomb shelter in the basement of the school, with concrete benches on which our small grade-school bodies fit like anchovies in a can. It was only used for tornadoes, which posed a more immediate and real danger, but tornadoes were not as scary as an atom bomb. We lived at the top of Tornado Alley in the Midwestern United States, so we knew what to do in response to the air raid sirens screaming their warning of incoming winds. The destruction a tornado causes was therefore real and possibly avoidable if you had enough warning, unlike a nuclear attack, which seemed another level of destruction, hard to imagine and impossible to avoid unless you could travel to another time or continent. So we understood that nuclear war was a lot less likely, but potentially more devastating. I am sad that my own children have been trained to deal with a possible attack with an automatic firearm.

At the end of my grade-school years, our family moved to Ohio to a luxurious neighborhood as a result of my father winning a waste water management engineering contract with the city of Cleveland. We traded in one bathroom for nine people to six bathrooms for seven people. By that time the older siblings were heading off to college. With my mother's support, my father's business had gained the success that fueled the move.

The brick house in Ohio had a breakfast room separated from the kitchen, a bay window providing cheerful light on three sides. We had a front and back staircase, and my bedroom had red-and-white striped wallpaper, an ensuite bathroom, and a balcony, truly fit for a princess. Although I never found it, I believed the house must have a secret room somewhere. The only drawback to the Ohio house was that neighbors were very particular about their lawns and did not approve of our bare-footed abandon. And there were certainly no piles of dog poo.

I wrote notes to myself in pencil in various notebooks as a young girl, jotting a few lines then quickly starting new ones, being careful to put curls on the capital T and O in tidy cursive.

Nothing much has happened. Today we got our X-mas tree. I have soap in my ear — Love me I drew a happy face in pencil beside the fancy capital L, like a primitive emoji — *love me — happy face.*

My musings as I reached my tweens focused on feeling fat and worries about my clothes.

"I should lose weight only who cares. Oh well no one will notice anyway whether I'm skinny or not," I told myself. (I can admit it now, at medical school I was secretly happy about my grief-inspired weight loss — as if being skinny were worth the price of losing a loved one.)

In my teen and young adult mind, mid-nineteenth century female stereotypes loomed, making it increasingly hard to hear my core voices. One cannot turn back time, but I know now that in medical school I was trying to listen to that person who had been me in the past, the one who did not care and just wanted to move forward to her goals. Losing Ian meant not only was I finally skinny, but the price paid was the loss of a possible future with someone I loved. A future that had promised to look like everyone said it should — "first comes love, then comes marriage, then comes the baby in the baby carriage."

It has been more or less a chore in my life, as in most women's, to shake off these female tropes which cling like burrs on a dog, or interrupt your path like thorns in a thicket when you try to follow your dreams. These tropes show up with a glimpse in the mirror to see (falsely) that you're fat, or your shoes are bad, or, god forbid, you have 'bad hair', or any number of so-called transgressions, basically that you don't match the model on the shiny magazine cover. Like when I played goalie, and my mother asked why didn't I get to wear a skirt to match my teammates?

In junior high, the apex of tween angst, an ignorant boy taunted me on several occasions by calling me "nigger lips". This classmate targeted my looks even though I was as white as he was. Why he would use such a slur to taunt me I have no idea. I can only guess he had a difficult family with poor role models.

While digging into my old notes and papers, I found a seventh-grade, hand-written, five-page essay titled *My Life*. There is a giant grade of "C" written by the teacher in red ink on the cover page. It is a candid essay that suffers from repetition and grammatical errors, but is truthful and earnest, which to my mind should be more important than spelling. Years later I found another note in handwriting I did not recognize that read:

Ellen — If I was your maker, I would give you an A in life.

For sure, I'm giving myself an "A" — *happy face.*

In the 1970s, Minnesota high schools were just starting to allow young women to play competitive team sports. In 1972, the federal Education Amendments Act known as Title IX was implemented. "No person in the United States shall, on the basis of sex, be excluded from participation in, be denied the benefits of, or be subjected to discrimination under any education program or activity receiving Federal financial assistance," was the new state mandate.

For centuries women were not allowed to participate in sports; for centuries women were and still are expected daily to do hard physical labor to keep the home going: carrying water and children. Sports for women continues to be taboo in many parts of the world.

I was growing up on the cusp of this new era of women's sports. Katherine Switzer ran the Boston Marathon in spite of the race director trying to tackle her off the course. My mom bragged that she was the fastest runner in grade school, and talked about how her mom Veronica used to swim across the Mississippi River. I could see that my mom had been even more trapped by female stereotypes than I was, and I could see the possibilities as the world opened up to women athletes. I am also struck by the fact that Ian loved me even though I wore goalie pads instead of a kilt.

When I was in grade eight my family moved again, away from Ohio, as a result of my father's growing engineering consulting business. We settled into a lovely old home named Sunwood on the St. Croix River in Marine on St. Croix, Minnesota. Sunwood is just downriver from the climbing area at Taylors Falls where I later went rock climbing with Ian. The St. Croix River at our doorstep changed with the seasons and years; in winter it was like a giant Etch A Sketch — snow erased all the details of spring, summer, and fall for those dark months. Sunwood was the house with the wooden stairs in the black-and-white picture where Jenny sits on the step above us laughing, with one arm around me and the other around Ian.

The house was built in 1848 during the lumber boom, and reportedly was haunted by a poltergeist named Hiram Berkey. Hiram tossed cans off shelves that lined the old wooden stairs leading down to the damp dark basement where clear sparkling cold spring water ran in a trough. One day Hiram cracked random windows in the sun room while I was quietly reading in the summer light. No one knew why he haunted the house, although a common theory was that poltergeists centred on an adolescent girl, forming a field of emotional energy. I moved to Sunwood at age thirteen. At age twenty-four, Grief was my new poltergeist, fracturing me emotionally in lieu of breaking windows.

As a teen I explored the overgrown riverbanks visible from that sunroom, digging in the rich soil under the old flat moss-covered stones (part of a much older garden path) as if to uncover the happier days of childhood, but I no longer collected bugs. Instead, I read a lot of Harlequin romance paperbacks, apparently to reinforce those female tropes? Or perhaps to understand them.

Our village of Marine on St. Croix had just over five hundred residents. My "Marine people," as I nicknamed them in my head, were my friends who lived on the river, who rode the school bus to the next town for the years of junior high and high school. My best friend Nancy lived up the hill. She was number three of seven kids in her family. We spent endless hours on the river together, familiar with all the secret beaches and back channels, a watery version of my old neighborhood on Osceola Avenue. Marine People looked out for each other when I lived in the village and they still do.

"I was out cruzing around town and I saw tracks on the mill pond & they looked like KIDS there is open water & muck, the kids would not last long if they fell threw so talk to them please! ice rescue is not a good out come!" reads a 2018 social-media post from a long-time Marine on Saint Croix resident.

I have to admit that as a tween I also left dangerous tracks on the frozen mill pond near open water. We also "cruzed" the St. Croix river in a flat-bottomed duck boat in late spring, the ice just breaking up; we skipped the boat up onto the ice and pulled the motor up to turn the boat into a sled until we reached the next patch of water. I don't believe we wore life jackets.

Water, snow, and ice are always irresistible and, as I learned later, also incredibly dangerous. Memories of Ian unleash landscapes of snow and ice, ski slopes, snowfields, alpine snowcaps, where biting cold winds take your breath, with a soundtrack of the crunch of boots or the scraping of metal-edged skis carving a perfect turn. My high-school memories are of cross-country skiing and racing, hours on the snow every day building a solid base for running and hiking in later years.

Summers were spent drifting on the river, on canoe trips in the boundary waters, the Quetico, and once a trip on the Kazan River to the Canadian Arctic. Even now, I kayak, canoe, and paddleboard whenever I can. Whether beach or mud or stony slopes, whether ocean, stream, pond, river or lake, water spilling onto shore speaks to me in calming rhythms.

Considering my past also means remembering the two times my nose was broken. The first time, I was a young child. Carrying my dog down the concrete stairs leading out from the kitchen of my Aunt Mary's tall, old, lake cottage I fell onto a wooden bench at the bottom. The cottage is set into a hillside at the edge of a lake in central Minnesota. My mother looked at my crooked nose and simply shoved it back into place. That was that. My siblings called me "worm lips" and "elephant nose" for a good part of that summer. I guess I never did consider myself a dreamboat. The second time was in grade ten. I was thrown from a horse to land crumpled in the grass after bouncing off a white woodshed, fracturing my hip, messing up my face, and breaking my nose again.

"You might need to go to the hospital, but my mom told me not to use the car," my teenage friend said to me as I lay in the dirt with blood pouring out of my nose.

This reminds me now of the way the medical school responded to my request to delay my start after Ian's death. Rules are rules, and there are no exceptions, even if you are lying in the dirt with broken bones and a bloody face, or if your beloved has just died. My parents weren't home so someone called an adult neighbor to take me home to Sunwood. I recall staggering into the living room to lie on the couch.

"No, no, don't lie there, you'll get blood on the couch," my sister Meg said.

As I crawled to the floor, she said, "No, not there, you'll get blood on the rug." So I managed to make my way to the wooden floor of the dining room, where I lay with my head safely on the kitchen linoleum. I think that's when my little brother (sibling number seven) came down, took one look at me, freaked out, and fled upstairs to lock himself in his bedroom.

Finally, another neighbor took me to the small, local hospital. When my parents got home they saw the blood in the kitchen.

"Where are Meg and Ellen?" Mom asked through my brother's locked door.

"I can't talk about it," he replied.

I'm not sure how my parents finally got word that I was safely at the hospital, but I learned from this chaotic incident the lesson vital to responding in a crisis, medical or otherwise: "first of all, take your own pulse." If you freak out, you can't help anyone. But I suppose it's also about temperament; some people are probably naturally suited to certain professions.

After breaking my nose and my hip riding bareback on an unfamiliar horse through an unfamiliar forest, which was great fun until it wasn't, I had surgery to reposition my nose. The bruising on my face and the limp from the hip fracture lasted several weeks. Good friends in school were nice to me, but others were not so nice and made fun of my bruised face and limp. Somewhere in my teen years I also got kicked in the face with a skate. I was playing tag with Dave, a neighbor kid, skating on the frozen St. Croix river when he fell and his foot flew up cutting my cheek with the blade. It got infected and that side of my face was as big as a grapefruit for a week. My teenage years were not too pretty.

My peers in the village during those years did not spare sneers nor mince words about appearance. "Brown Spot" referred to a girl with a large chocolate-coloured oval birthmark on the back of her right thigh; "Four Toes" was a girl who had lost her big toe in a riding mower accident when she was a toddler; and "Zit Face" was an unfortunate, red-headed boy. Such nicknames were tossed around without inhibition, with the recipients acting as if they didn't care. While I didn't use these labels, I didn't speak up against them either. The ones mocked stuck together without any apparent ill feelings toward those mocking them, but I still remember the hard words. Perhaps I didn't speak up for fear of being called "Melon Face" or "Gimpy".

It is tempting to say I wish I could go back to my childhood, but what would be the purpose? The problem with going back in time is that time still moves forward. And if you could freeze yourself in a specific wonderful moment in your life it is likely the novelty and enjoyment would wear off; all your favorite things soon would become tiresome or irritating. Imagine cuddling your precious child or favorite dog forever — you might need a break no matter how cute they are. Also, you cannot go back and choose an alternate future. Which parts of your life today would you chose to lose? A bad job? What about those friends you've made along the way, children you have had, or your current pet? As with Aurora, who forgot to ask for her mortal spouse to be eternally young, eventually your life would become untenable; Aurora eventually decided to turn her beloved into a cicada. My forays back in time do remind me that I was and am part of a family and community, that I knew how to be happy and optimistic about the future, and that I am no longer a child.

Ian had pointed out the problem of hindsight. I look for clues in our last week together. Should I somehow have known? Should

I have been more careful? That last week is, in fact, unremarkable in my memory; all the packing and unpacking and gear sorting in the living room, working at the grocery, eating Grape-Nuts in the kitchen, all blend together. We climbed and hiked, putting miles on our feet, adjusted our boots and applied moleskin on our blisters and hot spots, packed and unpacked again, and prepared for the next adventure. All these things we did, our routines, were well worked out by mid-summer; we were happy in a calm way, and purposeful in our short-term goals. What if I had a tesseract to go back and see that last week, or maybe stop it? For what purpose? Maybe is it better to say hindsight be damned and trust that I will write and re-write my memories to keep the love in my heart. Regardless, the past cannot be changed no matter how hard you try.

This is not the story of my childhood, but about the messy stuff that got piled on later. I was that little girl. Under all the years of experiences, I still am. That little girl held me up in the late summer and into the fall of 1986. She was like an ant holding up a giant green leaf or like a tiny dung beetle that rolls another dung ball uphill after the first one gets stomped on. I look back to find the younger me again; she still had things to teach me, including 'don't get soap in your ears'. *Love me — happy face.*

At the end of summer, 1986, I had traded the majestic Cascade mountains for the colourful fall leaves and ten thousand lakes of Minnesota. I rediscovered the joy of the river, experiencing, after my loss, a kind of baptism in all that is pure and sweet. Returning reminded me of the flow and snow of winter, spring, summer and fall in the upper Midwest.

heavy lifting —————

MUSCLES
AND FASCIE

THAT FEELING OF BEING DROPPED OFF AT A REMOTE
LAKE WITH A FORTY-TWO DAY JOURNEY AHEAD.

fig. 4–1

DISSECTION

——— ———

unburied truth

I was just weeks into the cadaver months when the glacier on Mount Baker chose to dish Ian and his companion in death back to the surface like a pet cat offering up a dead bird. There was a call, whose details are erased by time, to tell me Ian's body had been found. Grief grabbed me by the shoulders and slammed me backwards into the pit yet again. My hand grasped the receiver, the far-away voice through the telephone adding to the sensation of falling as I listened. Sometimes through those old telephone lines you could hear the distance the sound had to travel. Sometimes the voice was particularly clear: "It sounds like you're right next door!" This particular call sounded as if it came from millions of miles away.

Years earlier in Alaska, when I was working as a maid over the summer break from college, the summer Ian sent me the "crushedly yours" letter, I went whitewater rafting on the Nenana River.

"Hang on," the guide shouted as we headed towards a standing wave in the rapids.

I happened to be sitting at the bottom of the "v", the exact spot the raft folded when the front of the raft hit the wave. The boat bounced me out and the water yanked me into the rough rapids. I tumbled backwards underwater, my body like a sock in a full load of laundry during the wash cycle, and only because I was wearing my life jacket did I bounce to the surface, sucking for air. Tumbling under the water with no idea which way was up was terrifying. That call from Washington State about the body being found was just like being torn out of a raft into rushing water with no chance to catch a breath — I was back in the washing machine.

One evening a few days later, I sat at the antique, round, maple table in my parents' kitchen, back home at Sunwood in Marine on St. Croix, talking it over with my mom and dad. The old-fashioned light above the table made of retrofitted gas lanterns softly highlighted the worry lines on their faces.

"It's not a good idea for you to go back right now," my father counseled me.

"I have to go," I insisted, my mind made up. "I know you think it's stupid. I'm sorry." I knew that my father, like the rest of the world, wanted me to just put that Seattle chapter, including Ian's death, behind me and concentrate on medical school.

"I don't think it's stupid," my father said, surprising me.

"Really?" I replied, relieved.

"I think it's worse than stupid."

I knew, even at that time, that his words were from a father's heart; he was trying to protect his child from further harm.

So, stupid or not, I flew back west. Ian's family welcomed me as if I were family. They had lost a son and a brother, and I had lost…what exactly? Boyfriend wasn't really the right title, neither was fiancé or husband, perhaps pal, or sidekick, or common-law partner? Perhaps lover, loved one, or beloved soulmate? Ian and I were never engaged officially, so I had no family status except through their goodwill. What did it really feel like? It felt like I had lost part of my own body — a limb, a rib, my heart — with Ian's death.

In a small room in a small town outside of Seattle, we viewed his body. Seeing Ian dead was confirmation, hard but not as shocking as his death. Ian was still himself, a slightly blurry version, his features smudged like a pencil drawing gently effaced with a gum eraser. More freshly dead people, ones you know, are harder to understand as being dead, like the Sierra fish before the evil smelling fixatives take effect. The air in the room smelled like moist paper towels with a lemon wedge, maybe an olive thrown in; the scent of Ian's body after a month under the snow was not so bad really. My imagination could have created worse. The damp odor surrounded us in the confines of four walls.

"Do you want to keep the boots?" one of the staff asked.

I remember saying, and perhaps his family saying too, that we should not take his boots; he might need them for the slog of eternity. I kept the navy-blue fleece that had been patched earlier in the summer after one of us burnt a hole in the arm, his ice axe, and other items that were given to me at that time, including a watch which was still working. The old Timex slogan "It takes a licking and it keeps on ticking" popped into my head when I saw the watch. If only Ian had been a watch.

Ian's family decided that he was to be cremated, not buried. I cannot linger in my memories here too long as there really are no words to describe this so private and final moment. Ian's cremated remains reduced to about the size of a shoebox, unexpected, but at the same time making sense in a way because we are all mostly water, the ashes chunky with bits of bone, fine gray in colour, soft in texture. How can it be that this small collection of matter was once a living person I loved?

The day Ian's family chose to return him to the mountains was another warm, clear, summer day in the Cascades, like a scene in a tourist postcard. White mountains contrasted with deep-blue skies; a green slope in the foreground showed rare pops of red, yellow, and lavender from fading, late summer wildflowers. The group of us hiked silently into the mountains, with no idle chatter about weather, route, gear, or food. Just steps on the dusty trail, stopping at a familiar ridge to throw those bits and pieces that were Ian's remains out into the landscape, ashes fluttering to disappear in the alpine grasses. This time I hiked back down under my own steam. What more is there to say about this? It had to be done, on top of everything else. These memories are detached, like images behind frosted glass, the final parting. Step. Rest. Step. Rest. Repeat. Repeat. Repeat.

Ian's family not only included me in all the preparations, invited me to accompany them to his final place on the mountain, but they also generously gifted me the small amount of money he had in his account, which I used to have a garnet pinky ring engraved with "in memory of Ian." When I picked up the ring, the jeweler had made a mistake, the inscription reading "In memory of Ia". "Ia" would have laughed. Of course, they fixed it. Years later, I lost it twice, once on a beach in the sand, finding it after searching, the second time in the snow on the driveway of the house where I was living at the time. In the spring, after the long Minnesota winter, it suddenly appeared again in the thawing snow. The pinky ring was eventually stolen in a break-in. My magical thinking tells me it is out in the world somewhere, perhaps still on its way back to me.

My first brush with death was as a small child of around four, meeting my great-uncle Charlie in his coffin in a small, old, wooden church outside of Hinkley in central Minnesota. The chapel so old it must have survived the great Hinkley fire of 1894. For some reason my siblings were not there; my parents only took me along to Uncle Charlie's funeral. His old-man body was displayed at the front of the small congregation. I was curious and unafraid. The door behind us at the end of the central aisle was open to invite any late arrivals. It must have been summertime.

My next encounter with death was after graduating high school in 1980, on that 625-mile canoe trip with a camp group on the Kazan River. We finally beached our canoes on the shore of Baker Lake (also known as Qamani'tuaq), then located in Canada's Northwest Territories, but now part of the territory of Nunavut. The town of Baker Lake / Qamani'tuaq is a hamlet of about 2,000 people located on the shore of the 728 square-mile lake, at the approximate geographic centre of Canada. The canoe trip took forty-two days and we did not encounter any other human outside of our six-women group. This was a horizontal adventure of vast unoccupied sky and earth stretching to all horizons, a precipice laid flat. We had the privilege of seeing a massive caribou migration across the endless tundra. For days the large mammals paralleled the Kazan river, first as specks on the far horizon, then coming closer and closer until one day our path was crossed by a river of large, brown animals that seemed would never end. This is my benchmark of wilderness.

At the end of our journey, there was a layover for a couple days at Baker Lake / Qamani'tuaq. Rows upon rows of old, gray shacks stretched back from the lakefront, with the one hotel, the Iglu, simply a Quonset hut. A young man rushed up on a quad and abruptly handed me an orange with a smile, which was very strange; I now realize it was an amazing gift from this local, since everything had to be flown in and fresh fruit was at a premium. We had a couple days before our scheduled flight out on a "Calm Air" plane, so I went for a run around the town to pass the time. (I have to point out the irony of the airline's name as the winds were fierce.)

I ran to the graveyard, the only destination on the gray gravel road that stretched for just a few miles in each direction along the treeless shore of Baker Lake, where the bodies were in boxes above ground because of the permafrost. This method of burial is similar to the graveyards around New Orleans, which are built high off the ground because of water, except instead of glorious stone mausoleums, here there were only wooden boxes with the lids covered in pebbles. Feeling it disrespectful to run through a graveyard, I slowed to a walk. Rustling began all around me as if all the bodies in their boxes were shifting, moving around, and coming back to life. It took a moment for me to recognize the sound as a very light rain starting to fall on all those pebbles, like wind in the air around me rustling through dry leaves.

Freshly dead and related dead are just like that, pausing at the threshold of death as if they will spring to life again at any moment, as if they are still in the in-between. Following my whispering experience in that arctic graveyard, steps from the shore of Baker Lake, death next met me on the slopes of Mount Baker.

I returned to Minnesota after my trip back to the Cascade Mountains to put Ian to rest, and went straight to the administration office to sort out scheduling details since I'd had to miss classes. The taste-lessly decorated office featured textured wallpaper, burnt-orange carpet, and ugly Formica left over from the 1970s.

"So how did it go with your dead friend?" that same matter-of-fact administrator called to me from ten feet away in front of other people.

"Okay," I mumbled, confused as to the proper response with the gallery of administrative staff eyeing me, all curious to see what I would say. These decades later I ask myself if I am remembering or mis-remembering such callousness through the veil of loss, but there are numerous studies in peer-reviewed literature demon-strating that in medical school cynicism increases and empathy decreases. This trend continues through residency and beyond. It may very well be true that the physicians who were leaders in the medical school administration at the time were not capable of showing compassion, that they had been hardened over time like diamonds created by intense pressure. These professionals were, and still are, created by the pressures of a damaging medical training system. Forget the pain and the past. Focus on the goal. Don't be stupid. And don't forget to cultivate your game face. The medical school curriculum stops for no-one. It is all very matter of fact and get on with your work — many caregivers are unable to care.

I was so hyper from trying to keep up with the volume of facts and medical school tasks, I was like a hamster racing flat out in a wheel. I could hardly stand to write anything by hand, but preferred to type letters, or notes, or sometimes journal entries on my old typewriter because typing was faster. I folded the entries into the pages of my journal. I ran from place to place because it took too long to walk. I typed about waking up with a crystal-clear image of high camp at Mount Baker in my mind, from the vantage point of that last ridge above the treeline about two-thirds of the way up, high camp on a jutting plateau just to the right and above, with Mount Baker cloaked in snow to the left.

One morning just as I awoke, I remembered my dream — Ian about to leave for the climb on which he was killed, I telling him I loved him and asking him if he loved me, he with that impatient air that he always had before a climb. I asked him many things, but did not tell him not to go, in spite of the fact that I knew he would be killed. He was killed. In my dream, someone had his body and would not give it back; finally given the body, I woke up.

Day and night I bargained with my memories, trying to rewrite my story so as to have a happier ending. A Romeo and Juliet part of me believed it would have been better if both of us had died rather than either be left alone. This is the logic of loss, an objective hazard of grief that must be traversed to find hope.

I buried myself in Ian's clothes that I had kept in my closet for months. His unwashed clothes were an olfactory archive, sadly fading over time. Perspiration is a language of human emotion and a personal signature, as time spent in any university library, clinic waiting room, job interview site, or running, climbing, or at any other physical pursuit proves. From sour stress sweat, the bane of dress shirts, to the sweat that captures the salty aftermath of exertion. I grieved Ian's smells.

That fall my older sister Nancy, number two in the family, had a baby girl, her third child. One day she was over to visit with the baby, chatting with me while her older child Ross, then just a toddler, played on the stairs leading up from the kitchen. Wistfully, I watched him put a colander on his head, laughing at his own antics.

I needed a counterbalance to all my bleak ruminations. There were many days I lost my battle with grief. I was all alone even with others around me. The flip side was sometimes suddenly realizing I was alone. Growing up in a large family, I escaped into my books, but I was rarely actually alone. Training for cross-country skiing as a teen and young woman I did spend hours by myself on the trails, but I did not yet recognize these experiences as solitary because it was in service to a team. I went right from the big family to college roommates to Ian so I never did cultivate my solitude. Later I was so lost in my own head it didn't matter if I was physically alone or not. It has only been after a long time and a mindful practice that I've started to enjoy being alone. Being alone does not mean being lonely. A peaceful walk in the woods, a restful read of a novel in the bath, or making your cup of aromatic coffee in the morning can all be pleasurable moments alone.

The counterbalance to my bleak thoughts was a list I kept in my journal. A concrete list of gifts from Ian: skills of climbing, mountaineering, sparkling bioluminescent tides, Northern Lights over the mountain, downhill skiing, and fixing my car. The counterbalance reminds me always to take any hypotenuse I find, to be accepting of what fate demands, and to remember joy. Recently I hiked from the south rim of the Grand Canyon to Phantom Ranch on the Colorado River, over four-thousand feet down and back up, with precipitous, hundred-foot drop-offs at the edge of the trails. Suddenly I heard Ian's voice murmur another of his Ianisms.

"You don't fall into the street when you are walking down the sidewalk, do you?"

This was his way to encourage me to walk forward without fear.

"You can't go back, don't let it hold you back," people kept repeating. "You must move on to new things."

"Yes, thank you," was my stock answer. What I really wanted to say was, "Please shut up. You have no idea what I am going through."

There really are no right words to speak to a griever, although even badly phrased words in an attempt to comfort are better than no words. From a practical standpoint, "That sounds hard" or "I am sorry for your loss" might be better choices than "you must move on". Also keep in mind that grief often steals the griever's manners.

After returning Ian to the mountains, I went back to my skull and cadavers. I put my head down as I was advised to do and powered forward. I focused on each step, one at a time, and the medical school curriculum provided a rigid path. There were no choices to be made at that time. Follow the program or sink into the earth. So, I followed the program. There was nothing else to do. Step. Rest. Step. Rest. Repeat. Repeat. Repeat.

ON MOUNT BAKER SUMMIT WITH MOUNT RAINIER IN THE BACKGROUND.
WHATEVER IAN IS SAYING TO ME HERE IS MAKING ME HAPPY.

fig. 4–2

DEEP FASCIA

———

but for fascia we would crumble to bits

Ashes sifting through fingers and fanning out over the alpine meadows brought some solace. If only following the rituals and tasks of death meant there was no more grieving left to do. In my core, I still struggled to believe that Ian was dead. He had existed and he existed in my memories. Grief came and lay beside me each night, a quiet and gentle grief. We were like two cadavers lying side by side in the cadaver lab, perfectly still and forever silent.

I was struggling to keep on task and failed a biochemistry midterm. The professor, aware of my situation, was kind enough to let me re-take the exam, and I passed on the second try. The northern days were getting shorter with more hours of darkness as the months advanced. Winter loitered around the corner. I was spending more and more time drifting back to August and the alpine slopes. Spending time with Ian in my memories.

"I know you don't believe in the traditional concept of God," I tell him. "But I think we can agree that there is an amorphous spirituality shared between humans. It's like the deep fasciae that connects, protects, and surrounds the muscles and tissues in the body. Spirituality is the deep fasciae of souls."

"I guess you are learning something after all. See I told you— you've got this," he says.

"Yes, maybe, after all, we've always been debating whether one could prove or disprove God, not about whether God exists or not."

As we walk along the trail, I continue, "It seems like spirituality is a concept developed in the face of an unacceptable absence of purpose in human existence. Life is just a vigil awaiting death."

"That is seriously oversimplifying things," Ian points out. "That is the problem of hindsight, remember?"

"Humans are just an unfortunate product of random evolution. Unfortunate, because we are intelligent and have self-reflection. Macbeth was right about all the tomorrows creeping in their petty pace like a multitude of curses, as if taunting the living who are left behind with the knowledge that all the years ahead that stretch out in endless days add up to nothing."

"On the other hand," Ian reasons, "who's to say that the spiritual realm doesn't exist?"

"And you're not going to tell me?"

He raises an eyebrow and gives me a teasing smile. "I think it's different for everyone. It's a definite possibility though."

"Just because I would love to be sure that there was some higher purpose, that your death was for some actual reason and not the result of a random geologic phenomenon, doesn't make spirituality true," I insist.

"Sure," he says. "Feeling that your fate is held in higher hands would be comforting, yes, and it might help your anxiety for the future. After all, if you believed, then you would trust there was a plan for you outside of what you can comprehend. But you can't force yourself to believe."

I shake my head, "Well, it seems most likely that I will just always be anxious and never really accept that such a plan exists."

"You can't predict the future," he says, smiling. "You know that."

"What about this. What if we gather all the heavenly beings together for a celestial tea party? Invite them all—from the God depicted in the paintings in the big St. Luke's Catholic Church in St. Paul, to the Greek and Roman gods and goddesses, to the Muslim prophet who cannot be pictured, to the Hindu gods and goddesses, to any and all deities we can think of. The Spaghetti Monster can come and perhaps his eyes would be meatballs because for a deity real eyes are most definitely not a necessity. We can spend eternity questioning them all, and drink from Russell's tiny celestial teapot, perhaps we would just have to trust that the tea was there. Maybe, given enough time, a pure form of god would be present in their overlapping thoughts. It would be like the Mad Hatter tea party crashing the last supper."

"That's an interesting idea." Ian laughs. "I think a more methodical approach might work better? Aren't you supposed to be the scientist? But who's to say? Throwing the world's deities in a room with snacks might be fun."

While I did not manage to find God or gods, glimmers of respite appeared in the corners of my dark mood which were mirrored in the lengthening nights. I still talked a lot about Ian to those around me, in spite of the incessant advice to "just move on". It seems I needed to tell my story; perhaps speaking it out loud helped me understand it. I talked about the mountains, and it was lovely to recall so many happy moments with Ian. I talked about climbing, its intensity, the smells and sounds, the routines, and the rewards, the rope whirring past you and snapping to a halt, the click of carabiners securing the rope, the smell of sweat and sun-soaked skin. As I spoke, I felt myself dangling my feet over a tiny ledge five-hundred feet off the ground, the wind whistling by our exposed perch, and felt the balance, strength, grace, and concentration it takes to climb well.

Grief also spoke to me, "Now that you are dust, realize that you have been dust before and probably will be dust again, and then dust finally. So, take your time. Feel what it is to be dust for a while, slow to rise, admire the view of the sky from your lowly place. When you are ready, gather your strength, reconstitute the self that cannot be destroyed, gather all the pieces from the floor and be stronger than before." Grief lay on the floor with my broken pieces, saying, "I have faith in you."

In December the first sugary snow once again filled the sky and covered the ground with shimmering crystals that reminded me of the Northern Lights and the phosphorescent tide. It would have been Ian's twenty-third birthday. I had managed successfully to finish my first med school exams, end of term one, year one, with many to go. I was proud of myself, but also terribly tired of being serious, and deeply tired of being haunted by grief, although I was slowly making peace with her. We were becoming unlikely friends. What I needed was a trashy novel to read (but maybe not a Harlequin just yet).

In February, 1987, Reuters reported that an avalanche near Breckenridge, Colorado, killed three skiers: Martin Donnellan, twenty-one years old, of Peekskill, New York; Paul Way, twenty-three, of Auckland, New Zealand; and Nick Casey, twenty-three, of Cambridge, New Zealand. It feels important to name them and not just call them "avalanche victims," which seems to be the custom in many reports. They were not just three of many caught by the snow in a given year, but three individuals whose lives were lost and whose families were thrown into the maelstrom of grief.

When the press coverage flooded me in the aftermath of the Mount Baker avalanche, I called Ian's brother Brett, who was working in Vail, Colorado, at the time, finding his voice a comfort. He told me that all the news reports brought back difficult memories for him as well.

I was whirling in the mix of grief and medical school; most days were filled with too much coffee, too much pain, and too much studying. Insomnia visited almost nightly — it felt better to just stay awake to escape the nightmares. If tears are the sweat of sorrow, I was toiling hard. I wished that grief came with a finite number of tears. Then I could count them to know when the pain would stop.

I have to pause here to acknowledge the massive number of deaths in our ongoing pandemic that started in 2020. There are still deaths from mountain avalanches, but the deaths from COVID-19 mean that these few avalanche deaths no longer make the news. But all deaths impact family, friends, partners, and those who are trying to save lives — mountain rescuers and front-line medical workers alike.

We are facing a tsunami of grief. So many lives lost, it's unfathom-able. The waves of grief will reach out from the families of the lost to those who tried to care for them for years to come. I hope with my writing to offer an open hand to lift them up, help them to learn to live with grief. It is possible to live with grief — there's the hope.

By the spring of 1987, intense despair had morphed into a more chronic sadness that felt like a cold, gray, moist blanket. Grief was still my constant companion. I was participating in a grief-recovery group that a fellow student had suggested. All women, we met in a nondescript room in the basement of a hospital where plastic chairs were set in a circle on the tattered and worn light-blue carpet. There were no windows and a single easel with a large pad of paper and markers was placed next to the leader under the fluorescent lights. During one meeting the leader drew two overlapping circles to illus-trate the griever and their lost one, then erased one entire circle leaving a crescent remaining, a former circle with a big bite taken out of it. All of us in that room were grievers, were no longer whole; we were a room full of crescents. A group of like-minded crescents who could readily see the missing parts.

What we did not say to each other was, "Try to get more sleep." That would have been seriously laughable, and most of us would have either snorted aloud or quizzed, "Did you really lose a loved one?" Sleeping, too much sleep or no sleep at all; eating nothing or everything; bathing or not bathing — these are the ADLs, the almighty Activities of Daily Living, the benchmarks of sanity. Forget it. Grief steals your sanity and your ADLs. We could see in one another the drowning griever. To be dressed and in that room was to be commended. This community of folks with fresh losses was validating in a way that no psychologist could be. We knew the pain, the dysphoria, the feeling that the future was lost. We could say to one another, "Yeah, I too sometimes believe it was all a bad dream."

The stories were compelling.

"My husband was a fire fighter and would come home and hang his coat in the front closet," one woman explained. "It sometimes smelled like smoke. I keep thinking I smell smoke."

Another tearfully told her story, "About a month after my boyfriend was killed, I drove home from work and saw the police, and my trailer had burned to the ground...I had left my dog in his kennel before I left for work..."

"They would not let me return my wedding dress after he drowned," said a young woman with long, dark hair who had lost her fiancé just a week before her wedding. "He was diving in a limestone quarry as part of his work to clean debris from the bottom and his tank malfunctioned. The dress was never worn — they should have taken it back."

This community of truths allowed each of us to recognize our own individual grief, and to be reassured that each grief follows a unique and meandering path that will eventually lead to the future. In the group all losses of loved ones were treated equally. In the real world it seems sometimes that people try to rank losses, that certain deaths are more tragic than others. A child lost is believed to be more grievous than the loss of a reckless adult driver, cancer in the young more unbearable than in the elderly. Suicide or overdose deaths are avoided by most people in conversations. Which is worse, death of a spouse or divorce? Estrangement of a family member or the death of a family member? And what about those who take risks like mountain climbing — is that less devastating because they were taking a risk with their own lives? If you are the loved one left behind, your grief is as large as any other; your heart is as wounded as any other broken heart, no matter the cause or circumstances. The true love of any human for another is equal regardless of the relationship, as is the depth of loss.

We agreed too that the symptoms of grief can feel crazy. Many of us would pick up a telephone and hold it to our ear before remembering that our loved one was dead. We all looked at the front door expecting our lost person miraculously to walk in and say, "I'm home." Many of us had nightmares if we could sleep, and insomnia for the remainder of the night.

Step one for many of us was simply to feel sad and know that what we felt was shared by others. In grief, we were in the depths of winter, the season of short days and bitter cold silence that coats the earth in darkness. During the winter of grief, fighting is fruitless; waiting and resting are the keys to surviving until spring.

What I have only just understood recently is that grief is like your own personal fairy godmother, as important, but not always as delightful. Grief never leaves, so you might as well make friends. I decided to name my grief "Mabel." Although a person doesn't "get over it" when they lose someone they love, it is possible to make peace with grief. Mabel is still here decades later, like a bossy old friend waiting in the background ready to take on the next loss, whether big or small, so the old-fashioned name suits her.

Don't fight your grief, just tuck and roll, slide on your back or flat on your face for as long as it takes. Eventually your grief will be there to carry your history, to remind you never to forget, and to remind you that you can raise your head to see the light that exists outside yourself, and know that light exists within yourself, even when it seems you have fallen into endless darkness. It seems my Mabel is not so bad after all — to the round house, Mabel!

I AM NOT CHANNELING THE PILLSBURY DOUGHBOY WITH MY THROW-
AWAY GARDEN GLOVES. THE START TO THE 1987 TWIN CITIES
MARATHON, MY FIRST AND FASTEST MARATHON. IT WAS COLD
ENOUGH FOR ICE ON THE PAVEMENT UNDER SOME OF THE BRIDGES.

fig. 4–3

ACTIONS

---

you can run (and run) but cannot hide

I began running regularly again. I ran and ran until my toenails fell off. I ran until my fingers turned into little sausages with shiny skin from fluid accumulating. In the winter, I ran until my eyelashes froze together in the bitter cold. I ran to soothe myself. I ran until I forgot the miles I covered, forgot I was even running, as if the past and future might disappear as well. It was as if I was one of those ink perspective drawings where the road disappears at the apex on the horizon. I ran to remember and to forget. Feet hit the earth or pavement with each step. The footfall transmits the force through ankle, knee, hip, core, shoulders and head. Through blood vessels, arteries, through breath. The arm and contralateral leg swing in anticipation of the next footfall. Repeat. Repeat. Repeat. Breath and feet reach a détente that allows many miles to unfold.

One magical thought I had was that if I ran far enough, I would end up someplace else, reaching an alternative universe in which no tragedies occurred. I first started to run as a teen to get in shape for cross-country skiing. I also lifted weights in high school, which was not considered very ladylike in the 1970s, even though the Title IX amendment against gender discrimination in sports had just been enacted.

"You walk too athletically," my mother told me, trying to help me become an acceptable woman for the times, which was also the reason she later hoped I would wear a field-hockey skirt.

"Too bad if someone doesn't like the way I walk," I replied.

In high school, I was blessed to live within walking distance of the William O'Brien State Park, which had miles of wooded trails. In winter after school or on the weekends I would put on my cross-country ski boots, throwing my skis and poles over my shoulder, and walk up the hill to the trails where I could ski twenty to thirty kilometers without repeating a circuit and more if I wanted to do a few laps. Once into my rhythm, I flew on my cross-country skis across the snow without attention to the effort involved, floating over dips and curves through pine forests, the smell of snow and wind in my face erasing everything but movement; this was my version of flying—flying through the forests. I didn't know why this was such a joy to me. Now I understand that it was moving meditation through the trees.

Running can never compare to gliding on skis across groomed trails in the tranquility of winter, but it can have the same rhythm. St. Paul and Minneapolis have lovely neighborhoods and trails around lakes that made for varied routes during training runs, particularly beautiful in the fall with the trees flaunting their gold and red to the stately old homes along the banks of the Mississippi.

In the footsteps of Katherine Switzer, I finished my first marathon the following fall, 1987. The route encompassed the River Road beside those mansions, and the marathon fell on a perfect autumn day with a temperature about freezing at the start, the only hazard a skiff of black ice under the first few bridges. The crisp air and friendly crowds pushed me to what was my personal best. I've never run a faster time and I've run a marathon almost every year for decades. And contrary to Ms. Switzer's doctor's warning, my uterus did not fall out.

The marathon distance of 26.2 miles is reportedly based on the ancient story of Pheidippides who ran from Marathon to Athens, Greece, to announce the war was won.

"Rejoice, we conquer," he exclaimed, before promptly dropping dead, or so the story goes.

Running marathons is an exercise in biochemistry, my medical school, basic science courses were teaching me; too little water, too much water, too many electrolytes, too few electrolytes, simple carbs, complex carbs, the list goes on with miscalculations in the dance of fluids that takes place during a lengthy race leading to cramps, dehydration, or diarrhea. There are thirty-thousand to fifty-thousand steps in a marathon, such counting reminiscent of calculating how many steps it would take to climb a certain mountain. Too much water, water intoxication, causes a dangerous low sodium condition called hyponatremia, and, according to studies, runners' diarrhea. These "runners' trots" might be caused by hyperosmolar gels, meaning the sugar and electrolytes in the gels and liquids consumed will draw excess water into the gut.

Other theories blame the jostling of internal organs for speeding up the gut.

In long distance events, the body first uses up fast fuel in the form of glucose, then medium fuel glycogen, then the slower source of energy from fat, before finally running out of biochemical fuel, and hitting the wall, which is also called "bonking". The wall is unpleasant, but in spite of best planning it is sometimes unavoidable. There are many variables that play into a good marathon result, including training, sleep, nutrition, and injuries, not to mention weather conditions and temperature on race day. As a new medical student training for a marathon, I spent the first several miles pondering biochemistry and physiology, the next miles drawing on the larger questions of where my life was going and where it had been, then after many miles my focus settled solely on my feet, my breath, and the rhythm of the road.

As I ran each marathon, I modified my goals. I had a time in mind if I was having a great race, a fallback time in mind, an "I'm glad I finished" goal, and then a promise to myself never to be carried off the course in an ambulance if there was any way to avoid it. I also vowed not to run with a poopy butt after seeing that in a fellow marathoner, who, whether from gut jostling or too many electrolyte gels, had succumbed to the runners' trots. Finishing a marathon is a great feeling, but to my mind not worth risking injury or indignity. At the end of each race, whether fast or slow, it is always exciting to run through the chute under the big clock with everyone cheering even if you are the thousandth person to finish. You feel like a superstar when a volunteer places a finisher medal around your neck; then you are ready to relax for the rest of the day.

Years later I put my body to a big test. We runners were lined up to run the Grandma's Marathon in Two Harbors, Minnesota. It was hot and very humid. I was running with my brother Paul, number seven of seven. We agreed we would run at our own pace. At the starting gun we were off, a blissful mass of humanity, like lemmings on a crazy quest. Then about mile six a woman in front of me slowly fell forward like a bird from the sky, her arms flaccid behind her, her chest hitting first and then her head. She fell in the unusual heat and humidity, and I took a long leap over her and then stopped. Her head was in the ditch on the gray gravel, her body draped on the pavement. There was a tiny fraction of a second where I calculated the effect of stopping on my final time, but I knew I had to help the woman in the ditch. She was lying on her side, so I checked her pulse and breathing. Other medical professionals stopped to assist.

"Don't move her, her neck might be broken," a woman said.

"We need to make sure she has an airway," the next man on the scene exclaimed.

All the while the mass of humanity that is a marathon continued to run by.

"She's turning blue!" a runner yelled.

This was true because by that time she was having a seizure and we tried to support her neck and airway.

"I don't know CPR," another runner yelled.

"I am a general surgeon," said the next runner on the scene.

"I am an epileptologist," the next announced.

An epileptologist, I thought, a seizure specialist — perfect! The patient was by that time stable and in good hands, so I excused myself and continued, now very much behind any planned time I might have had for that marathon, although I still could finish under my own steam and not get diarrhea. Towards the end of the marathon, I encountered a man who told me he'd had a stroke earlier that summer. I shared my electrolyte sport jelly beans with him.

Around mile twenty-one we ran into Duluth. A woman was standing, contorted from muscle cramps, in the middle of the road. There were no official medical personnel in view, so a fellow runner and I performed a two-man, four-hand carry and brought her to the side of the course and then found medical professionals. Minutes later I came across a male runner proposing to a woman runner. They required no assistance. I sprinted to cross the finish line exactly five hours after starting and declared for myself a personal best for first aid assistance in a marathon.

Recently I watched *The Secret Marathon*, a documentary film based on a book by Martin Parnell, which tells the story of a marathon he and the Afghani filmmaker ran in her home country. Brave Afghani women joined the marathon and ran for equality and freedom. How lucky I am to have no barriers to running or other outdoor sports beyond my own motivation. A few years ago, in support of Martin's Right to Play efforts, I signed up for and played a forty-two-hour-long, continuous soccer game in a gym outside Calgary. In fact, our team earned a *Guinness Book of World Records* certificate for participating in the world's longest indoor soccer game. Running and other sports build confidence, improve mood, and have so many other benefits. Run and walk if you can, your body will thank you with good health.

Running in the winter requires a special skill set. You must alter your stride to slightly shorter and wider steps in order to be ready for a slip or slide — more specifically you try to run like a penguin. You must dress appropriately. My rule of thumb is if I can stand outside for about one minute and not feel cold, then I have on the right number of layers; if I am immediately cold, I am underdressed;

and if I don't start to get cold after a minute, I'm overdressed. Being overdressed is a nuisance: excessive sweating leads to being damp then cold; and peeling off layers leads to having too many things tied around your waist. Going out underdressed you risk frostbite in frigidly cold temperatures; every gap needs to be covered — wrists, ankles, neck, and face — to ward of the icy wind. In extreme-cold running I tie a scarf around my face, a tiny slit open between scarf and hat to see, my breath soaking and freezing the scarf into bumpy rough fabric that rubs on my nose, my eyelashes freezing together by the end of the route. The best method to unfreeze lashes is to gently press them with your bare fingertips, once it is safe to take off your mittens. Running in winter is a perfect distraction from grief because it requires a lot of preparation and many adjustments along the way to avoid frostbite. Another pandemic aside is that face masks also keep your face warm in winter.

You must also know how to fall on ice. If you run in the winter, you will inevitably fall. The key is to become entirely limp, succumbing to the momentum of the slip and fall, tuck, and roll. Do not try to catch yourself with a hand, arm, or elbow because you will break a bone; ease into a fall like a filet of Lutefisk smoothly sliding off a spatula onto a plate. (Lutefisk is dried fish soaked in lye then boiled to produce a gelatinous texture, a favorite of Scandinavian descendants in Minnesota, mostly served at church holiday dinners, especially by Lutherans. It slips down your throat with no swallowing required and smells like the inside of a well-used running shoe.) Once you've hit the ground and skidded to a stop, obey your first instinct: get up quickly and look around to see if anyone saw you fall.

The shortest daylight of the year in Minnesota is eight hours and forty-six minutes long; the pavement is covered in snow, ice, and darkness by the time school or work is done, by the time you have a spare hour for a run. But for me it was worth all the preparation, learning the skills and the risks; exertion chased all thoughts away with every breath, and sometimes running was the only way I could get the hamster off the wheel in my brain.

Ian and I had spent a lot of our time together skiing, climbing, hiking, and mountaineering, with training runs on the soft dirt trails in the lush woods of the Carleton College arboretum, through the varied forests that included burr oak, hawthorne, birch, pine, and trembling aspens. I once ran through the fields and paths near Beatrix Potter's home in Near Sawrey, in Cumbria, England's Lake District, while traveling with Jenny the summer before Ian died. Potter's seventeenth-century stone home with slate roof and surrounding random stone walls is named "Hill Top", and is just as lovely and cozy as the homes her bunny characters live in. I navigated all kinds of gates that swung open, up, down, or sideways, each with a different type of latch, up and over little staircase stiles, hopscotching through the sheep pastures. Jenny meandered on her own and we'd meet up afterward, eager to share vignettes we had collected along the way. The lush and rolling hills looked like perfect bunny habitat, and as I ran I imagined Peter Rabbit with his little blue jacket cavorting among the nooks and crannies of this pastoral landscape. Jenny might easily be another invention of Beatrix Potter with her whimsical imagination and flowing sundresses. These are the memories that still keep me running.

After the avalanche, running was a means of escape, and now running is a solitary, meditative part of my life, or sometimes an opportunity for socializing. Recently I went on a short run with my sister, two nieces (one the niece who was born the year of Ian's death) and a nephew. The years have stolen much of my speed, but not the satisfaction of finishing a long or short route, whether alone or with friends or family.

In addition to trying to outrun grief, I also bought a dog that year after Ian's death. Dogs have been family companions for as long as I can remember. A shaggy black mutt named Andy was one of my first memories. And my father has always had a brown-and-white, female, Springer spaniel, inevitably named Dixie, even into his nineties. While I was traveling in 1985 and 1986 it was not practical or fair to own a dog, but now, with at least a four-year stint ahead in medical school, a dog seemed a given.

Loup, pronounced "Lou," was a Belgian Tervuren sheepdog who looked like a cross between a German Shepherd and a Collie, with a loyal disposition and lots of hair, burnished brown with black tips, and black mascara markings from the corner of her eyes. Loup is the French word for wolf. When she was a tiny furry baby, I tried to have Loup sleep in bed with me, but she favored the floor next to the bed, waking me up in the morning by standing to rest her muzzle on the pillow, her moist, black nose almost touching mine. I would open my eyes nose-to-nose with Loup's face, humid, dog breath gently blowing onto me. No other dog has done this until my most recent pal Ed, a Pyrenees and Australian Shepherd mix, who just recently started waking me up like this, his dog breath on my face.

Loup was quiet, not growling or barking much, just standing to stare at the door if she wanted to go outside. She had me trained, which I figured out after my parents looked after her for a few days at Sunwood. My mother noticed Loup standing in the corner of the kitchen by the door for a couple of hours and thought it odd behavior, but did not understand that Loup wanted to go out until Loup finally just peed on the floor.

Random things like pots and pans in the kitchen cupboards spooked Loup; she never walked over grates or sewer covers on the street or sidewalk, and she liked to dig large holes in the backyard, as if she intended to come out on the other side of the world. Loup was also a master at getting food off the counters if no one was looking, once managing to grab a whole pie in a glass pan off the counter without spilling the pie or breaking the glass; I found the pan licked clean in the middle of the kitchen floor. Tupperware posed no problems either. Loup peeled off the covers without leaving any teeth marks, devoured the contents, and always left a clean container. I read that hot peppers could deter dogs from stealing food, so I once left jalapeno peppers scattered across the counters. The first day, there were bite marks in a few of them, next day Loup ignored the peppers but still took any food that was left out. Needless to say, Loup was a good incentive to keep the kitchen counters clear.

As the new year unfolded, I consciously sought out activities that brought me comfort—my running, Loup, talking to myself in the mirror to remind myself I was still alive and to comfort my reflection, long baths, and spending time with friends, my large extended family, and the grief group. I spent less time trying to will myself into the earth, and more time reviving old habits like buying flowers for my new home in Minneapolis, which I shared with my sister Jeanne, the third oldest in our sib group. Seasonal, sweetly scented, light or dark purple lilacs were added to the mix of store-bought bouquets. Grief seemed to approve of my strategies, but continued to be a constant companion, a spirit shadow always in the background.

Because the bathroom in our apartment in Seattle had been tiny, with only a teensy shower next to the tiny sink, I had lost the habit of nightly baths. A lingering soak in a hot bath at the end of a long day is a good thing, with science supporting the urge to heat your body in a tub of water, by calling it passive warming. According to studies, a hot bath is equivalent to thirty minutes of exercise. In addition to burning calories, passive warming reduces blood pressure, improves mood, and improves sleep. These were not facts I learned in medical school, because that science came out later. I just knew it felt good to be still in that very warm water and so I revived the habit. Baths were and still are a break in the day where no one will interrupt, and these days no electronic device can hound me with notifications.

The bath is a sacred space. Each tub has its own personality, including the capacity of the hot water heater, the bathing ritual depending on the infrastructure. Certain tubs demand you run just the hot water to achieve the perfect temperature since the water heater is small; other tubs require you to carefully balance hot and cold to perfect the soak. My favorite is still simple water, no salts or bubbles, only the feel of hot clean skin without the residue of perfume or oils, the heat giving the body a buffer against cold northern nights, and a reason to welcome winter with warm flannel pajamas.

Writing was also a solace. Like taping bugs to the kitchen floor, the act of putting pen to paper or fingers to keyboard gives some control over the winds of life (or at least the illusion of control), as if once a thought or event is on paper it's okay for you to move on. I started writing early, in my childhood notebooks, and I understand why journaling is popular. In the journal I kept intermittently after the avalanche I mused as to why we feel the need to remember. What purpose does it serve? Would it not be better simply to forget the pain of separation by denying its existence? Just like Dave and Ian's ice axe debates, my debates with Ian had been a game, a pastime whereby each tried to persuade the other to come over to their side of the argument, as if agreement would mean we'd found the truth. My debates with Ian continued in those journal pages and along the alpine paths. I wondered if I was just debating myself, but knew Ian was/is still there.

It was always late in the day by the time I wrote in my journal, something other than studies catching my interest, like an idea for my next trip or sometimes something more mundane like a sudden urge to clean the refrigerator. I put all of my photos into an album one night in January 1987 (this was before the explosion in of digital photos and online sharing), arranging each three-by-five matte colour photo onto the sticky album page, smoothing the clear plastic over each montage, reliving the past years of my life, my friends, my Ian, with — in the words of an old German friend — one laughing and one crying eye. In spite of all the miles, my baths, my Loup, my friends, and my family, I still had nightmares, the nightly apparitions morphing into my present life events. Ian no longer haunted me daily, but Mabel stood quietly in the shadows.

PART V

THE NERVOUS SYSTEM

flight, flee, freeze, or frenzy

HEMISPHERES: IN THE BIOCHEMISTRY LAB.

fig. 5-1

THE HEMISPHERES

―――――――

which is smarter, head or heart?

My second year of medical school started in the fall of 1987. I was almost a live human again, ready to say goodbye to the cadavers and set death aside for a while, at least in my daily life. I was slowly able to focus on the outside world again. I joined the medical school Phi Chi coed fraternity. Some of the members lived in the brick house across from the medical school, which became a kind of meeting place for residents and non-residents alike. In between classes we would hang out in the living room or kitchen, or play foosball in the rec-room, and of course there were parties after exams were over.

One evening I met a graduate student from a different faculty while out with my med school friends, and wrote in my journal that night *Well, I'm not much in the mood for writing except to say I was charmed tonight by a fellow who bought me a rose!*

That fall I met Dick (a nickname I gave him), a first-year medical student who lived in Phi Chi. It was at first a casual friendship — a few foosball games, coffees, and walking to classes together. Good looking in an all-American albeit nerdy way, Dick hailed from southern California. He had neat, short, straight, dark hair, a preference for bow ties, and a smile showing off nearly perfect teeth. He was an expert in thirteen-lined ground squirrels, having written his Master's thesis on that rodent, a rodent that was also the mascot of our school: we were supposed to be the Minnesota Golden Gophers, but apparently "Goldie" is not in fact a gopher, but a gopher-like, thirteen-lined ground squirrel, which Dick proudly pointed out to me one of the first times we met. As the fall term passed, we spent more time together and before long I was spending nights with him at the fraternity house. We enjoyed going for walks and had the shared goal of a medical degree. It was a light and easy partnership.

A few months into our relationship, Dick's parents came from California for an unexpected visit. I didn't know they were in town until we woke up in the morning to a fellow frat member knocking on the door to say they were outside the house.

"Stay away from the window!" Dick hissed as he scurried to put his clothes on. "I haven't told them about you yet!"

I stayed out of sight as requested, while he called down to them through an open window from his second-storey room.

"I'll be right down!"

Dick later explained, "I would like them to have a good introduction to you. It would have been an awkward way to meet them."

"That's reasonable," I reluctantly admitted. "Should we plan a brunch or lunch?"

I was formally and properly introduced to Dick's parents at breakfast at the local Key's Café on Raymond Avenue in St. Paul, where the sticky sweet rolls are freshly made and the size of a dinnerplate, and the hash browns and eggs are piled high. His mother, whom I later secretly nicknamed "Wedge" due to her seeming always to be pushing Dick and me apart, was a sturdy woman with a large bosom (possibly her bosom has grown in my memories) that preceded her into any room she entered. Dick's father, thin and quiet, had a wan smile perpetually on his face. It is also possible he has shrunk in my memories. Upon meeting Dick's mother, it became clear why a more formal introduction to her was the best strategy, and I felt relieved that they lived in southern California and not Minneapolis. I hung back to leave a larger tip on the table.

In spite of the short walk to class, I still held my breath each time Dick walked out the door in the morning if I was not going with him, sometimes peeking out the window to make sure he made it across the street. A splinter of fear that had not been there before had lodged itself in my heart as if all life was a tenuous fiction, threatening to evaporate at any moment. I couldn't help being reminded of sitting by the window at the Yale Street apartment watching the empty street darken into night when Ian had been late to return from Mount Rainier. The difference was that Dick was only walking across the street, not climbing one of the highest mountains in the lower forty-eight.

Dick and I liked adventuring in his tan, VW Westfalia pop-up camper van, exploring small towns and out-of-the-way destinations on breaks from school. On one of these trips the Northern Lights put on a swirling show above the shores of Lake Superior. There she was again, Aurora, painting the North Shore night sky with luminescent green, blue, and white.

We headed up to the North Shore again for the smelting run later that year. Rainbow smelt are an invasive fish species introduced to an inland lake in the early twentieth century. They found their way into Lake Superior, and by the 1970s smelting season, the annual spring smelt run, had become a local event, as thousands of fish moved into the streams along the shores of the great lake. Dick and I were catching the end of the smelting heyday when tourists, including us, travelled to small towns in the area to participate in the annual fish fries. Restaurants had all-you-can-eat specials of breaded deep-fried smelt that were tasty and paired well with the local beer. There are still smelt along the North Shore of Lake Superior, but they run in smaller numbers now due to conservation efforts and ecological changes. Months later we vacationed for a week in a house by the ocean in Southern California, spending hours listening to the waves and the ocean breeze, a breather between medical school and the future, a moment to just be together.

Dick was a skilled woodworker specializing in fine carpentry and furniture building. He taught me about dovetail joints, that were the same hand-mitred joints that made Skull's wooden box so lovely. We moved in together as I was going into my third year and Dick made a bed and a pie-safe with vented doors. Our place was a ground-floor apartment in an old, white, wood-sided house with a sagging front porch a few blocks from the medical school. At night, large white slabs of paint, most likely containing lead, peeled off the kitchen ceiling, slapping softly onto the linoleum floor. I listened from my bed and it sounded as if someone was gently tossing magazines onto the kitchen floor. Every morning we took the short walk to school through the park under tall hardwood trees. That house reminded me of a decrepit bride, like Miss Havisham in *Great Expectations,* waiting in her fading finery among the stately oaks that guarded the house with their own decaying beauty.

A few months later, we bought a Japanese fighting fish, its purple fins wafting like feather fronds in the clear round glass bowl that we kept on a white wooden shelf that rested on the Victorian-style, painted radiator in front of an old, multi-paned window.

Some months after we bought our fish, I went out of town for a week or so. Back home, I noticed there was something different about the fish.

"Something is wrong with the fish," I said to Dick as I paused from making dinner.

"Hmmm," he replied.

The next morning, coffee in hand, I sprinkled a few flakes of fish food into the bowl, put my face right up to the glass, and peered in to watch the fish swim.

"He looks sick," I insisted. "He isn't moving right."

Dick finally blurted, "Alright already. It's a different fish. I changed the water and forgot to let it sit to evaporate the chlorine before putting it in, and the other fish died."

"But why didn't you just tell me?" I asked, genuinely puzzled.

"I don't know," he said sheepishly. "I just felt bad because I told you I would take care of it and then I killed it."

Almost finished my first two years of basic science courses, I applied for and was accepted into the combined MD/PhD program. School dished up endless tasks to keep me busy along with like-minded colleagues with a side of fun, so there was no reason to rush to the finish line. The idea behind a combined MD/PhD program is that a physician scientist needs both research training and clinical training to successfully pursue medically relevant research. Eight years on average, on top of a four-year undergraduate degree is the investment it takes, and the majority of MD/PhD graduates end up in academic centres with the aim of being involved in research throughout their careers.

The difficulty is to find time for both clinical medicine and research within a finite number of hours in a day and also have a life. This problem does not reveal itself during the first years, when focus alternates between the two and when you look up it is already night. Only in later years does it become apparent that hours in the lab mean fewer hours at home and for loved ones, and even fewer when medical clinic duties are added into the schedule. A benefit is that research can be absolutely fascinating—like solving a puzzle over a number of months or sometimes years.

Stacene was a fellow MD/PhD colleague. She and I enjoyed spending time together and still do as often as possible on my Minnesota visits. A tall redhead with a big smile and a bigger intellect, Stacene's specialty was microbiology and, later, pediatric infectious disease, which she topped off with a Master's in Public Health. Iowa roots ground her and she has a deep acceptance of others. Her small, second-floor apartment provided another venue for medical school parties, one of which resulted in banana peels on the ceiling fan. We practiced giving presentations of our research, mine on the biochemistry of kidney basement membrane proteins and hers on bacterial microbiology, each counting the other's "ums" and "ahs" with which we unconsciously seasoned our speeches, like placeholders. Talking too fast was another sin in timed presentations; it was an art to include all the pertinent facts within the allotted minutes while speaking at a measured pace. In early 2020 through to 2021, Stacene was my pandemic forecaster.

"Is this a real thing? Should we be worried?" I asked her in January 2020.

"Wait and see," she told me.

"Should I stock up?" I asked her in February when health officials advised people to have on hand a two-week supply of food, and a month's worth of toilet paper.

"Yes," she said. "Stock up now."

"The fall and winter, the shit's going to hit the fan," she told me.

Stacene continues to be both a friend and a great source of solid information.

During my second and third year of the PhD research portion of my program I started climbing again with another fellow MD/PhD student. Shane was a careful, super-smart man with a ready smile and friendly eyes. In good weather we spent time top-roping at Taylors Falls, upriver from Marine on St. Croix, where I had climbed with Ian when we were at Carleton College together. During the winter months, Shane and I went to indoor climbing gyms with other local climbers, including his good friend Mikey, pronounced Mike-ee, who was an enormous, athletic man with surprising agility. It seems unlikely that Mikey was as big as "The Hulk," but that's the picture that comes to mind. He must have weighed at least twice as much as I did or possibly more than twice; while belaying him I would have to anchor myself to the ground with webbing and carbiners in the back of my climbing harness to avoid being pulled into the air if he fell. Mikey was twice as sweet as his size.

It was relaxing and satisfying to be out in the woods again, playing on the face of a cliff with a pal. It was a reaffirmation of both the sport and of my introduction to that sport by Ian. A good climbing partner, like a running partner, is a treasure, like the friend who comes over for coffee while you clean the house. Early one morning, Shane and I sat on the top of a climb looking down over the valley and the St. Croix river, which was exceptionally calm with tall trees whispering in the slight breeze; the serenity of the morning surrounded us. This was a step to finding my stride between old friends and new friends.

In 1988, Dick and I moved to our second rental house, on Bayless Place in St. Paul, and the following year I bought the house next door for $58,000, a large amount of money at the time. I do not recall why the old woman who owned the house had decided to sell, but she just put up a piece of cardboard on the front lawn with faintly scrawled words in pencil "House for Sale." There were no real estate agents involved. My dad came over to look at the house with me before I made an offer.

"As long as both the seller and the buyer agree that it's a good price then it's a good price," he advised me, and my next journal entry recorded my enthusiasm:

> So what if I'm living on a shoestring budget (more like
> a thread at this point) I bought a house!!! It was built in
> 1889 (stuccoed over sometime since) white, two storey, two
> bedrooms, front and back porch, small garage (more like a
> shed). We move in July 26th. Pretty exciting! I won a young
> investigator award with distinction from the Academy of
> Clinical Laboratory Physicians and Scientists. I flew out
> to SUNY at Stoney Brook, Long Island, and presented my
> research to more than 200 people. Then I goofed around
> NYC with my little bro Paul. We had a good time.

Bayless Place is a cul-de-sac about a fifteen-minute drive from the medical school. The house was exactly one-century old and had two, beautiful, tall, catalpa trees in the yard, possibly planted by one of the first owners, all of it enclosed by a white picket fence. In spring, the white catalpa blossoms fell like snow to cover the grass; in late summer long, brown, bean pods decorated the branches. The catalpa trees reminded me of Jack and the Beanstalk; they reached high toward the clouds with gothic branches and large, deep-green, heart-shaped leaves like hands to offer supplication to the skies. On the alley behind the house, the ancient garage was covered with tan and brown, asphalt shingles; an old wooden door took up one whole wall and swung easily open by hand; the lower half of the opposite wall had been extended so a modern car could nose all the way in. The original structure, of course, had been sized for nothing larger than a Model-T Ford.

The dirt in those gardens was thick and black as far down as you could dig, or as far as Loup could dig. The beds were filled with classic, old, nineteenth-century plants left by previous gardeners, including lily of the valley, iris, tulips, mums, and large fan-like ferns. I added more red, pink, and purple tulips, and huge orange, yellow, and red Asiatic lilies to have a supply of cut flowers for the house. Of course, there were also lilacs, both lavender and dark purple, which are a staple of many old, northern, Midwestern neighborhoods.

That year, Ian's father Paul mailed a poem to me, which was later included in his self-published memoir of stories and poems. The brittle paper now is burnished with age.

To Ellen — A Red Sweater
His upward-gazing face 'neath a baseball hat,
Loping along in my red sweater.
He loved you Ellen, be sure of that,
With a love which grew better, yet better.

His life knew rain but mostly sun,
Naught but health and more.
And it knew your love and your fun.
And that I'm grateful for.

"The flowers are fair as you are fair"
His last day was joy, and the stuff
Of love and beauty. Two tents were there,
Not far apart, "but private enough."

Next morning he left to climb that face,
Not to come back, but to die.
On that route of that mount, at that time, in that place.
Why again Why just then Why's it him Why?

Never again will you hear his call,
Never again a letter.
You are left with naught but sweet recall,
And my red sweater
Paul

The four-pound red sweater and poem still live in my closet.

While I was still working on the PhD portion of the program, my high-school friend Nancy from Marine on St. Croix visited to keep me company. We drank coffee and chatted on my rare days off, leaving only a few hours to clean the house. After coffee, Nancy and I would mosey along the tree-lined streets by the university's St. Paul campus, in and out of the small shops, showing each other things we found that we liked in the jewelry and clothing displays. Once in a while we'd buy something, but both being on a budget, this was mostly browsing for entertainment.

"I finally feel like I am reaching that easy companionship with Dick," I told Nancy. "Even our sleeping seems less self-conscious."

Dick planted a pear tree in the front yard of my new house. The next spring there was a pear on this little tree and I was so excited, only to discover that Dick, with his twisted sense of humor, had tied on the pear in recognition of Earth Day. Dick also liked to make up names for people. The group of men who got together to work on old vehicles in the small town where my parents still lived were "the belly club" due to the large number of middle-aged paunches in attendance. He referred to my brother Pat and his wife Suzy as "Rat and Floozy," exactly the opposite of their real personalities. Dick's pet name for me was "Smellen." On Sundays Dick would stand at the front window of our house on Bayless Place facing the congregation that flocked to the church across the street.

"What a bunch of sheep," he would remark.

Across the alley, in a cheerful, yellow house, lived an elderly couple named Ted and Margaret Nachbar, which Ted pronounced "neighbor".

"We are neighbors to everyone," Ted introduced himself with a smile.

Ted was in his nineties at that time. He had immigrated from Germany and come through Ellis Island. He was shorter than me so must have been about five foot two or three, and Margaret was not any taller. They were avid gardeners, coming across the alley to inspect our efforts, giving advice, and offering bulbs or cuttings from their garden. On weekends they went to the local seniors' high-rise complex to "visit the old people." They preferred to stay around the neighborhood, and told us the last movie they had seen in a theatre was *The Sound of Music* when it premiered in 1965. Once, as I drove up the alley, I saw Ted standing on his roof cleaning his gutters, with one end of a rope tied around his waist, the other end threaded through a window into the house; he told me the other end was tied around a radiator inside the bathroom as a safety measure in case he fell off the roof.

"If you don't get killed in an accident when you are young, and if you make it through middle age without having a heart attack or other medical problem, then you will live a long time," Ted observed with his ninety-plus years to back it up.

Margaret watched *The Price Is Right* every day in her kitchen, while wearing her housecoat made of light cotton fabric with snaps in the front. She criticized everyone and everything in an effort to be helpful, which Ted took in stride, once in a while turning off his hearing aid as she went on a tirade. One day she came over to look at my garden. Horrified by the number of weeds, she quickly bent down to pull them, promptly passing out on the lawn. Dick and I helped her to her feet and called an ambulance. She instructed us to take her across the alley to her house before the paramedics arrived, insisting on changing out of her housecoat into proper clothes for the ride to the hospital. She was treated and released with no apparent harm, and I tried to be more mindful of my weeds for the rest of that summer.

I still had Loup at the Bayless Place house, and Dick got a rescue dog, an enormous Irish Setter named Mike, who was freakishly tall, with long auburn hair, and routinely jumped up on the dining room table, all four paws and seventy pounds of him, and sat there. Maybe he wanted to be at eye level with the rest of us. I never did figure out why he did that, but it was awkward to have guests over for dinner. If he stood on his hind legs Mike was taller than me; he'd jump up and drive his front paws into my chest with enough force to knock me over if I didn't brace myself. It wasn't so much of a greeting as a challenge. I had sympathy for him, but not enough to tolerate being physically bullied, so I would flag out an elbow or a knee to avoid being pummeled by him. Once in a while, I stepped on his hind feet if he did that. As a result of my relationship with Mike, I would never again get an Irish Setter.

For unknown reasons Mike would escape at every opportunity, jumping out of open windows, through screens, even leaping out a second-storey window. One time he ran away, as usual with me chasing him, and got to the end of the street and veered onto the off-ramp of the highway. That was enough for me. I refused to run into oncoming traffic so I gave up the chase. Luckily, we later found him safe and sound.

One winter, he escaped and was out all night in minus 25°F, and turned up the next morning with frostbite on his pads. For days we had to carry him outside to pee. He ate and drank lying down until his paws healed. Another time he went missing for at least a week. A woman found him and kept him in her apartment for several days before calling the number on his tag; when she spoke to me she referred to Mike as "Ernest." Weird. I suppose we were lucky he was returned to us, or perhaps Mike was the lucky one.

Mike used to fart a lot. Big stinky ones. He would toot and then whip his head around looking at his rear as if startled, puzzled as to where that noise and smell originated. He would get up to move away from the stink, then fart again, and look startled again. If he was having a gassy day, he would move all around the house like this, perpetually surprised by his own flatulence. Sometimes he would fart himself into a corner.

Wedge and her quiet husband stayed at our house a few times when they came to visit from Southern California. In spite of my cleaning frenzy before each visit, Wedge always managed to find fault. She'd casually run a finger across the TV screen to show there was a fine residue on it or rearrange furniture to show the resident dust bunnies hiding beneath.

"Perhaps you'd like help cleaning?" she would say, not pausing for my reply before launching into a full revamp and cleaning of the house.

On one visit she decided to rearrange my pantry. I will admit to not being super organized, laying blame for my disorganized dry goods on my busy MD/PhD training program.

"See how much better it looks?" she announced as she showed me her handiwork.

I managed to choke out, "Thanks."

Soon afterwards Mike got in there to rummage around, knocking food and cans off the shelves, covering everything in flour; this was a doggy crime scene, with no need to dust for paw prints. I secretly gave him a treat.

When we had time, Dick and I walked with the dogs, exploring empty lots, parks, and spooky urban spaces. We strolled around clumps of grass and dirt under the highway overpasses, sometimes encountering worn-out looking individuals lurking in the brush.

We also developed a hobby of scrounging in junkyards for parts for Dick's newly acquired classic, red, International Harvester Scout that he decided to buy even though he already had the camper van. The Scout was an original SUV, fun to drive, with parts only available from other old vehicles of the same make. Dick also collected old jars and bottles with a fondness for the mossy green and deep azure blues. All the while, we were both busy, between Dick with medical school, and me with my research and also volunteering with a cancer support group and with a grief group at St. Mary's Hospital.

As a result of my starting the research part of the MD/PhD program, Dick leap-frogged ahead of me into the MD part of the program. Even though he began medical school a year after I did, by 1990 he had only one year left in the MD program, while I still had the last two years of medical school curriculum ahead of me. The small joys of making a house together with Dick, Mike, and Loup, together with the companionship of old and new friends buffered the hard work. I thought that spring was finally here, and that Ian's death was behind me.

SUCH A GREAT FEELING TO BE ROPED IN ON A LEDGE,
HIGH UP IN A BEAUTIFUL LANDSCAPE.

fig. 5–2

CEREBELLUM

———

Finding balance

By the time I'd completed my first two years of PhD research on kidney basement membranes, Dick was moving forward in the standard four-year medical school curriculum, and my friends Stacene, Shane, and other MD/PhD colleagues in my class were finding success in their labs. I was not duplicating their success, although I was still enjoying the bench research. Bench research is another name for basic lab research, as opposed to clinical research, which involves live humans. Bench research is like a combination of cooking and detective work—pouring and mixing various concoctions, putting them through different tests to see what you get; it's a lot more fun if you can make a discovery, otherwise it becomes tedious.

The choice of research advisor will determine the project you will be assigned to, and choosing is a black art. Professors must have room in their laboratory for a student, the incoming student has to try to pick an advisor they feel will provide an interesting and successful experience, and the professor must see a spark in the new recruit. Having limited experience in research makes it tricky to make a good choice or to know if a project will succeed. As a result, although the initial stages of a project may seem promising, the thread of research often shreds to a dead end, a destination my project was fast approaching.

The combined program taught me the challenges of basic science research, not the least of which is that in order to discover something new, the investigator must essentially guess at what the findings should be in advance of an experiment. Sometimes a hypothesis, this educated guess, is correct and sometimes it is not, with more complex experiments increasing the difficultly of deciphering what is a true result, what is an artefact. A bit like trying to prove that God exists.

Bias is a sneaky thief of valid results; consciously or unconsciously, researchers make errors by throwing out data that does not support their hypothesis (an error that medical professionals can also make, as in "that lab result must be an artefact" instead of recognizing it as a clue). Rejecting a result as artefact when in fact it could be the true result, will lead to missing insights. The flip side is that artifacts can easily lead both the researcher and clinician astray. Einstein is credited with "Chance favors a prepared mind", and as it turns out sometimes the most important discoveries are found at the periphery of existing research.

While my own project was going nowhere, there was tremendous excitement in the research community about the discovery that bacteria living in the hot springs of Yellowstone National Park contained an enzyme that could be used for gene sequencing. This excitement fueled my desire to keep going in the face of a possible dead end. When Watson and Crick discovered the structure of DNA and the double-helix configuration in the 1950s, Thomas Brock was studying bacteria that lived at very high temperatures in naturally occurring hot springs. The common wisdom was that organisms could not live above a certain temperature, but, in 1966, Brock isolated a sample (later named *Thermus Aquaticus*) that lived in Mushroom Springs at a temperature of 73°C (about 163°F). Smart researchers, obviously with prepared minds, recognized the import-ance of Brock's *Thermus Aquaticus* in the context of the Watson and Crick discovery, and raced to develop techniques to further the study of DNA sequencing by using heat to unwind the strands.

Each DNA strand is made up of four bases that are arranged in triplets, called codons, combinations of which make up the language of DNA. In the process of trying to decipher genetic code, there were two major problems. One was that a single piece of DNA was too miniscule to study. As a result, a method called "poly-merase chain reaction" (PCR) was developed to amplify a single fragment into many copies, which could then be sequenced. Kary Mullis is credited with developing PCR in the 1980s and won the Nobel Prize in 1993. PCR used an enzyme called DNA polymerase, and here was the second problem: the heat needed to unwind the helix also denatured the polymerase, which prevented the enzyme from functioning to amplify the piece of DNA. Smart research-ers recognized that Brock's discovery of Taq-polymerase within *Thermus Aquaticus* solved the heat problem of unraveling the DNA into single strands for PCR application and amplification of DNA fragments.

This serendipitous intersection of molecular biology and field research by a microbiologist provided the basis for gene sequencing which is the core of forensics and medical genetics that we take for granted today — with television shows and news programs casually reporting DNA evidence — that was not observable or measurable prior to these discoveries. It is amazing how much science we take for granted in our daily lives — from cars to cell phones to electricity to solar lights, etcetera. Brock did not receive any award or financial gain from his part in this revolutionary discovery.

"Yellowstone didn't get any money from it. I didn't get any money, either, and I'm not complaining. The Taq culture was provided for public research use, and it has given great benefit to mankind," was Brock's opinion.

My MD/PhD colleagues used the PCR technique derived from that spectacular Mushroom Springs discovery in their projects, and their excitement gave me the incentive to continue a career in research, to press against the brick wall my own project seemed to be hitting. PCR technology has allowed for 2020's COVID-19 testing and vaccines to be developed at lightning speed. As a scientist I am impressed. I have lived long enough to see this thread of scientific discovery lead to the ability to test and vaccinate against this novel virus. As a human, and as one who has suffered through grief, I also see the collective pain that COVID will put our communities through. It's actually stunning to me that people are annoyed that they need a PCR test rather than a rapid antibody test for some things like international travel, since most people have no idea what either of those tests mean, nor the mountain of science behind them.

Another pivotal discovery and happy coincidence, one that would later influence my own career, though I did not know it yet, occurred in 1981. Scientists working on excimer laser technology for use in precision industrial manufacturing got the idea to turn the laser on leftover Thanksgiving turkey. Rangaswamy "Sri" Srinivasan got the idea while looking at his dinner plate on Thanksgiving and he and his fellow researchers at IBM's Thomas J. Watson Research Center in New York began to think about how the excimer might affect living tissue.

The developing procedure was applied to human eyes in the mid-1980s, and this led to the first excimer laser, photorefractive keratectomy (PRK) in 1985 to eliminate dependence on glasses. Millions of people since then have undergone laser vision correction using the techniques of LASIK and PRK, basically the same excimer laser technology as first used by Srinivasan to etch leftover Thanksgiving turkey in a lab. This became part of my career path, along which I have performed thousands of excimer laser, eye surgeries over the past twenty years. It seems the glued-in eye of my childhood donkey toy, the dissected cow eye, and the baby doll's blinking eyes foreshadowed my future profession.

Unfortunately, although famous and exciting discoveries in the biomedical sciences were inspiring all scientists, including me, my project was becoming a dumpster fire. And I was watching Dick move through the MD program right on schedule, which highlighted the fact that PhD programs like mine had no set schedule and were subject to the whims of academic research. Mine was a tough road ahead, a lot like slogging up a mountain, except in research there is no guarantee that the mountain really exists. The mountain top you see through the fog may turn out to be just a shadow in the clouds, dissipating the closer you get. An additional obstacle is that discoveries threatening the status quo garner powerful opponents who might be trying to move that mountain as you are struggling to conquer the summit. Galileo and Darwin come to mind as examples.

Centuries later, contemporary scientists are still fighting the same battles against similar opponents; climate change science versus climate change deniers is just one of many examples.

Scientific research beckons, but the challenges of heavy layers of academic, political, and religious inertia threaten to suck the joy out of discovery or derail projects altogether. Fighting for resources, tenure, and grants in academic research eats up much of the time that otherwise would be available for actual research, and the pressure to publish papers leads investigators to rush the process. "Publish or perish" is a dictum at odds with the true nature of any type of scientific research.

While it is true that a prepared mind will be more likely to recognize opportunities and prepare more accurate hypotheses — studies have shown that people who believe they are lucky will see the money on the sidewalk while those who believe they are unlucky will walk right by it — there is no guarantee that even the smartest, most prepared researcher will not be chasing shadows. A Master's or PhD student might luck into a project that is well underway in the dot-the-i and cross-the-ts stages to pump out three or four papers in a row during their time in the lab, while other students toil for years in the eddies of a troubled project before they accumulate enough data to publish and graduate. There is a rumor that PhD programs only let students graduate when they get enough gray hair and wrinkles to look like a full professor. Perhaps now that I am nearly sixty, I could get a PhD on looks alone, although maybe not, since my hair is not completely white.

By 1990, I was mired in an inspiration-sapping research backwater. The allure of finding treatments or cures for kidney diseases no longer provided the excitement to offset the daily grind of actual research.

What does a day in the life of a basic science researcher in biochemistry look like? Well, it's running polyacrylamide gels and columns (methods to separate proteins), and in my case it was sifting glomeruli out of crushed kidneys through sieves. For my research project on basement membrane proteins, I gathered cow kidneys sourced from a local slaughterhouse, diced them up into fine pieces to create a slurry which I then put through a series of finer and finer mesh until the glomeruli were isolated. Because heat denatures and destroys most ordinary proteins (except thankfully the Taq-polymerase), I sat for hours at a time on a stool in a room chilled to four degrees Celsius, surrounded by glass beakers of various liquids on stainless wire shelves. The room was the size of a walk-in closet and had a shiny metal door. Here I panned for glomeruli, by swirling the burgundy slurry of kidney juice in the sieves for what seemed like eternity to find the final gold, which were the intact glomeruli. Those hours in the cold room provided endless time to mull over my two-year-old relationship with Dick.

Lack of progress combined with my growing ability to see a future beyond grief, made me increasingly aware of the politics and obstacles faced by academic researchers. The infighting between our lab and an adjacent lab over resources was the nail in the coffin. I bailed out of the PhD program. It seemed pointless to me to even get an MS. In short, I decided that pure research and academics were not my calling. On the other hand, I told myself, it would be a waste not to package these two years in the lab into a degree. It was reasonably straightforward to tie it all up neatly into an MS — relatively easy. I still had to write and defend a thesis.

I wrote many papers for my Carleton College undergraduate program in a computer lab, typing out phosphorescent green letters on a boxy monitor connected to a monstrously large computer that skulked in its own climate-controlled room next door. The monitors waited patiently on their desks, a blinking green cursor the only indicator they were on. The first computer I used for word processing was the size of my bedroom, though the act of typing was no different than it is today on a laptop. The structure of a scientific paper has also remained the same over the decades.

The Master's degree felt like a failure to me at the time. It took years for me to recognize the lessons those hours in the laboratory taught me — how to think critically while interpreting clinical data or trying to discern if a treatment for a patient is working or not. Just as in research, every clinical result has potential artifacts. A prime example is the blood pressure cuff, which if too small will result in an artificially high reading. Any clinical result may be prone to artifacts that may cause a result to look abnormal or normal. Patients' treatment and health depend on recognizing artifacts. Sometimes the treatment of a chronic condition is a long experiment where one thing is tried, measurements are taken, with a length of time from days to months before new tests can begin or before patient symptoms can be the measurement of success or failure. Patient care must be approached just the same as any other research experiment. If everything and the kitchen sink is thrown at the patient on the first clinical encounter, it is impossible to figure out what is helping and what is not. Patience is required. Knowing how to analyze complex problems is a huge asset.

My detour into laboratory work in the last years of the 1980s laid the framework for my eventual profession, even if it seemed an absurd waste of time in the moment. Many believe everything happens for a reason, or, to channel Einstein, knowledge small or large, in the form of a degree or just an observation as one trundles through life, is important and sometimes critical in the really big discoveries. A simple chance and a prepared mind will gain the upper hand in the end. Life is a chain of chances and choices.

My personal theory of life is that each human enters life like a superball—with a direction, location, and velocity based on gender, country of origin, ethnicity, parentage, and a number of other fixed factors. On the way to adulthood, we sail through life, and as obstacles crop up (minor bumps or the hand of fate coming down with a wicked backhand), we drift or career off in another direction, and while we can never regain the original path, we still have the possibility to influence what direction we are headed. It is up to each of us to raise our faces and look around to figure out what opportunities exist on the new path. We will hit bumps or face crevasses. Chance cannot be controlled, but choice can. True grace is finding serendipity at the feet of chance.

As a result of my two-year deviation into the laboratory, I was one year behind Dick in the program. In 1990, after successfully completing my Master of Clinical Laboratory Science degree, I was ready to move into clinical rotations in the fall. Winter was once again on the horizon.

IAN IN HIS HAPPY PLACE.

fig. 5–3

THE SYMPATHETIC NERVE

———

put on your own oxygen mask before helping others

My first two years after Ian's passing were a cocoon of knowledge, as a result of hoovering in as much information as possible from lectures and labs. This would be a good time to take a side trip into death language. Using the word "passed" is a gentle way to broach death. Saying he was killed, he died, he was smashed under a ton of snow and ice then smushed for a month in a glacier is a more truthful way to talk to others. As most grievers know, the griever feels a duty to protect those around them from the scorch of sadness; it's almost as if grief is an infectious disease and contact with the griever may be fatal. That is the experience I had early on, even with that young psychologist — I felt the need to protect her, even though she should have been trained to accept strong emotion. My grief appeared to be harmful to others, although later I can see that grief is a gift that makes me strong in the face of loss. My grief also has given me the gift of empathy to others who are suffering losses — when you are finally and truly strong, you can provide comfort to others without dissolving into sadness. Like a strong hand that can lift someone up after falling, truthful grieving gives the griever the power to comfort without falling back into the pit of despair.

My grief, Mabel, taught me that admitting to emotional trauma is part of what needs to be done. Mabel punched me in the face for many months, until I finally stopped trying to avoid the realities of loss that were my historical truth. It was not until I admitted I was broken into dust on the floor, that I could make friends with my grief, and let my grief help me heal. So, those of us who have grieved and who are actively grieving can give a gift to those with new grief — we can offer a safe haven. You cannot heal if you cannot see the wound or feel the intensity of the loss. It's okay to be broken and lost, to just be with those feelings for a while, sometimes a long while, to hold space. You can't heal if you can't see the wound.

In 1990, I wrapped up my MS after a fifth and sixth year of graduate school. My convoluted path. Finally, I embarked on my last two clinical years of medical school that were dedicated to applying all the information absorbed to treating live patients. On the heels of grief, a mountain of study, then a new relationship, I became a metaphysical juggler, struggling for perfect timing to keep love, death, and learning simultaneously in rotation.

Bates, Frank Netter AKA "F. Netter", and *Gray's Anatomy* were the staples for medical students learning the art of physical examination. These were texts and experiences that Dick and I shared.

Before the days of electronic media these hardcover tomes promised knowledge in direct proportion to weight; publishers furnished them with robust covers, knowing eager scholars would wear them bare. Each three-colour, carefully inked illustration was an expensively printed tribute to the importance of the information portrayed. These books looked and smelled like responsibility. I still love my old, dog-eared books. Electronic books do not record the smudged fingerprints, penciled-in marginal notes, and coffee stains of a well-loved book, nor do they compare in sheer weight. The chemistry of that old-book smell is a combination of benzaldehyde, toluene, ethyl hexanol, vanillin, and other chemicals that break down ink, adhesives, and even paper over time. Books, like fine wines, take on notes (like old tobacco smoke) over time depending on the environment. The pages of my old medical texts give off aromas of study, sweat, coffee, and a hint of insomnia.

To kick off clinical rotations, students awkwardly practiced on each other, auscultating (a fancy way to say listening) and peering into ear canals, noses, and eyes. After that came the leap from being a member of the general public to having the privilege to ask a stranger, a patient, any number of personal questions, including details of their sexual and family history if it was pertinent.

To lay hands on a stranger's bare skin is at first a foreign action. Just as a registered massage therapist learns the art of draping to protect a client's modesty during massage, there are tips and techniques for the medical practitioner to follow in conducting a physical exam. Touch is so important for both diagnostic and therapeutic care. The contract between physician, medical student, or other health care examiner and patient rests on trust. We must have the patient's best interests top of mind at all times, and that includes patient comfort with respect to gowns and coverings, cleanliness and infectious disease precautions, and a sensitivity to any specific issues that may relate to their individual case.

"Who am I to believe I can address this problem?" is the first thing we all thought during those first clinical rotations.

At first imposters in short white coats, we learned to touch another person. With practice, it became more routine and the amount of information gathered through the physical examination grew with increasing finesse. Even a simple hand on an exposed limb gives information to the examiner. Dry skin of summer smells like the Arizona desert, part sun and part sand; sweet sweat without exertion tells another story. Skin is subtle, soft or rough, divulging secrets. Sometimes odors you cannot exactly put your thumb on, like the leftovers from last night's dinner, might draw attention. All the physician's senses when examining a patient inform the diagnosis.

The examiner must have courage to ask, if warranted, "What does your poop look like, how many sexual partners have you had, and do you have any discharge from any body part?" The examiner then must lay hands on the appropriate body parts in order to gather information relating to the chief complaint. Just as people donate their bodies for gross anatomy, there are patients in clinics and hospitals who agree to be examined by medical students. All are to be commended for the part they play in the development of skilled physicians. We have to start somewhere. The majority of patients are agreeable to letting medical students be involved in their care, and without these willing participants, it would be impossible for a physician to learn the skills needed to become an independent practitioner.

Third-year medical students proudly sported stethoscopes, reflex hammers, and tuning forks for testing hearing. These tools of the trade, along with the white coats, were proof we were doctors in training, our badges of honor showing the world our accomplishments.

Decades later, I had a patient tell me, "You aren't a real doctor."

"Why not?" I replied in my well-practiced, brief, and bland manner.

"You don't have a stethoscope."

I laughed, asking him if he wanted me to listen to his eye with a stethoscope, which oddly enough is something that is in fact done on very rare occasions. I told my staff about this encounter and they bought me a tiny stethoscope pin that I wear on the lapel of my white coat.

Our third-year stethoscopes were just like those the real doctors who already had their degrees carried, but the medical school coats were short, without the gathered waistband detail that would designate a pharmacist or a dentist. In the hierarchy of white coats, the long white coats were reserved for those who already had an MD degree; although a Master's student in the laboratory in those intervening years, I wore a long coat that not only said "Pediatrics" but had my name embroidered on it. I had a classmate, Steve, through my clinical years 1990–92, who was very jealous of my long white coat.

Steve was short-statured and meticulously groomed. One day he informed me, "When I graduate from medical school I am going to get the longest long white coat there is."

I imagined Steve parading down the hospital hallways like a diminutive Little Prince with his stethoscope around his neck and the longest long white coat trailing behind him like a wedding dress train as he proudly went about his rounds.

Unlike the first two years of medical school, where all the lectures and labs were in the same classrooms and buildings, the clinical rotation years three and four of the standard four-year program took place in different hospitals around the city. As a result, as these last years progressed, Dick and I were rarely in the same building together and mostly on different schedules, so we saw each other only in passing even though we were living together.

The language of clinical medicine is like alphabet soup. I remember from an early rotation the question, "Was it MI or an MI?" Mental illness or myocardial infarction. It makes a difference. So these abbreviations are convenient, but dangerous if you aren't careful. ED? Emergency department or erectile dysfunction. It makes a difference. Just like "up-rope" or "slack". No matter the venue, language is important, and sometimes shortcuts don't work unless you have agreed on shortcuts in advance. LOL, laugh out loud or lots of love, maybe both?

The interview is the beginning of all patient encounters, so in third year we started history taking with real patients, using the standard format SOAP — subjective, objective, assessment plan. *Subjective* is what the patient tells you; this part of history taking is a tricky task because many people quickly get off track. A patient might lead with something that happened forty years ago or veer off to talk about a friend or relative who may have had something similar. *Subjective* also includes the review of systems to determine if there are associated problems being experienced by the patient that they have not connected to their primary reason for coming into the office. The review of systems can uncover useful clues to a diagnosis, or might lead down the rabbit hole to numerous unrelated concerns.

Objective are the findings the examiner measures or records, such as blood pressure, bruising, etcetera; examiner bias or artefact might obfuscate results based on objective findings. *Assessment* is a fancy word to describe the diagnosis, or the differential diagnosis, which is a list of possible ailments. *Plan* is the recommendation for the next examination, testing, or treatment.

The first history taking and physical encounter I recall was with a thin, old, white-haired man at the veterans' hospital. He was visibly ill, cachectic (fancy medical word for thin or underweight) with poor colour, as if he was already a ghost. In a raspy voice he kindly agreed to answer my novice questions. I sat opposite him on a smooth molded plastic chair in a sparse room with clean white flooring. I wore my short white coat, having had to trade in my glorious, customized long coat after I transitioned out of the Master's program, which clearly made not an iota of difference to this dying man. I hovered my pen expectantly over the blank history form.

"So, what is your concern today?" I asked in a soft voice, uncomfortable prying. I knew that I could not offer any real help to him. I was not yet a real doctor, and he had a terminal diagnosis.

"Cancer," he answered.

It was metastatic lung cancer with a poor prognosis, yet he answered me patiently as I worked through my list of inquiries. It was surely no benefit to him to use his limited time left in life to provide practice in history taking to an unsure medical student. I felt bad that he had cancer with a bad prognosis. I reminded myself that cancer, like grief, is not contagious, so stop being afraid. He recognized my sadness for his situation and made an extra effort to be kind to me, comforting me, which I recognized as that backward grief flip that turns the griever into the comforter of everyone else.

Over the many years since, I have received such kindness from patients, although it's rare enough to catch me off guard. My supposed superhuman white coat almost convinces me that I do not need care from others, as if receiving care rather than just dishing it out is a physician's kryptonite.

"Your superhero logo is hidden on the inside, in the back of your white coat, isn't it?" a cheeky patient said to me recently.

"Sad to say, as it turns out, my white coat doesn't actually give me any superpowers," I replied, and we shared a good laugh.

Holding onto compassion without drowning in the parade of diseases and sometimes despair that become daily fare in medicine is like tiptoeing on a knife edge; care too deeply you will spend all your time wringing your hands in grief, while lacking compassion you are not giving patients good care; stumble and you will either fall or be cut. Care includes treatment of both physical ailments and mental conditions; stress and depression might be primary or secondary issues. If healthcare workers lose themselves in the psychological pain of their patient, they take on an unwieldy burden that over time will shift their focus from the patient to their own reactions to the patient's pain.

Psychiatrists and psychologists, in particular, are familiar with countertransference, where the patient may evoke feelings in the therapist that have more to do with the personal issues within the therapist than with the patient. There are often factors within the caregiver that might impact their ability to give good care; hunger, anger, loneliness, and fatigue will impact your ability to be at the top of your game. It may be possible to address the issue, such as eating to avoid being too hungry and trying to get enough sleep, but it's always helpful to simply be aware of your personal issues so you do not attribute your feelings to the patient.

My grief hangover impacted my ability to modulate my outgoing compassion. Medical school was like picking a scab open over and over; after Ian's death I registered a series of smaller griefs, an endless injury that seemed like it would never heal.

In 1980–81 *pneumocystis carinii*, a rare pneumonia, was showing up in otherwise healthy homosexual men in California. By the time my clinical rotations began in 1990 it was clear that there was a specific virus responsible for this immunosuppression that was leading to infections and it was also clear that blood contact, including through dental and other medical procedures, was responsible. HIV/AIDS was a relatively newly recognized disease that had crossed into the human population from other primates. There were no treatments widely available, so it seemed to be a death sentence. It was the number one cause of death for American men aged twenty-five to forty-four.

This was also the time of Kaposi's sarcoma, a rare skin cancer, with associated, unusual, opportunistic infections. In the past three decades, I have only seen one case of Kaposi sarcoma, but back then uncommon infections were cropping up in patients, creating fear in the hospitals. Some people were reluctant to care for affected patients in spite of universal blood and body fluid precautions in the form of gloves, gowns, and masks. In fact, at a lecture I attended years later, a physician who had been practicing at the time reported that there were doctors who refused altogether to see HIV/AIDS patients. In 1992 a peer-reviewed article found that for physicians in Los Angeles "36% have refused to provide continuing care for HIV infected patients and another 12% indicated their unwillingness to do so should such patients present themselves for care."

Many physicians in the midst of the HIV epidemic remembered the polio, tuberculosis, and 1918 Spanish influenza epidemics of the first part of the twentieth century that threatened every health care worker involved. Modern day examples are SARS, Ebola, and now novel coronavirus COVID-19. All these present a real danger to healthcare workers trying to help affected patients. The World Health Organization reported that healthcare workers treating Ebola are twenty-one to thirty-two times more likely than the average person to become infected. Statistically, infected healthcare workers are more likely to die from Ebola than those infected in the general population (a fifty-seven-percent fatality rate compared to a forty-seven-percent rate). Epidemics are smaller, more contained outbreaks, and pandemics are global outbreaks, but both involve human to human spread. Any novel infection, whether local or global, will pose an increased risk to health care providers.

New disease outbreaks, like COVID-19, hearken back to the Black Death of the 1300s—that catastrophic disease in the middle ages—with similar isolation and quarantine measures arising out of increasing contagion. The word quarantine refers to the forty-day isolation of ships before they were allowed to dock in European ports. Quarantine and isolation rooms with positive pressure ventilation are present-day measures still used to attempt to contain infectious disease. The separation of the sick from the well continues to be the most robust method of combating spread of disease. That and washing your hands.

For healthcare workers, infection-control measures such as universal blood and body fluid precautions, developed as a result of the HIV experience, help to mitigate the risk involved in the treatment of disease, but even with all the proper hazmat suits, respirators, and reverse-pressure isolation rooms, the risk is not zero. For the general public the simplicity of recommendations stands in stark contrast to complex hospital measures—wash your hands with soap and water and practice social distancing. Stay away from crowds and avoid sick people if possible. These measures have stood the test of time from before the Spanish Influenza outbreak in 1918 to the present day. For diseases such as SARS, strict quarantine measures are able to quash the emerging disease altogether. There have been no new SARS cases since 2004.

In the early days of HIV/AIDS the method of transmission was unclear, which increased anxiety for those involved in care of affected patients; this uncertainty had our third and fourth year medical students whispering to each other in the corridors about which patients might be infected. Discarding used hypodermic needles and syringes — "sharps" — was a recognized hazard. It prompted one of my medical school professors to point out, "The right hand is the enemy of the left." Which is to say that if you can avoid recapping a needle with the other hand you reduce your risk. This involves putting the used needle directly into the Sharps Container, or putting the cap on the counter against the backsplash and working the needle into the cap with one hand. Hold the sharp in one hand and keep the other hand behind your back.

My childhood fear of nuclear war was greater than my fear of tornados, even though in the Midwest I was far more likely to be injured or killed in a tornado. It is the same with the fear of infectious diseases. We fear the unfamiliar or the unknown more than the known. Sadly, in the midst of widespread fear about COVID-19, a tornado in Nashville Tennessee killed twenty-five people and injured over one-hundred. You can bet that the majority of these people were more afraid of getting sick from the spreading virus than from the seasonal danger that lurks in the skies above. This is exactly why people become complacent about vaccinating against influenza, measles, or whooping cough, and now it's important to note that COVID-19 is far more likely to kill you or your children than Ebola. Diseases like measles are familiar, seemingly manageable because you might know someone who had it and survived, a dangerous line of reasoning. Vaccines were developed in response to the death and disabilities caused by these common infections. Even if these diseases are somewhat under control, that does not mean we can stop being vigilant and forget to vaccinate ourselves.

In the early 1980s, the HIV virus was identified as the cause of AIDS. It was not until 1987 that the first treatment, Zidovudine (AZT), was approved. Testing methods and protocols were still being developed, with a lot of uncertainty as to their effectiveness, which meant that HIV/AIDS was the plague of that time. In the early 1990s, medical students were not yet involved in HIV/AIDS cases out of fear of putting us at risk, which was fine with me. But this very safety precaution raised our fears even higher. The way we thought about this emerging disease was not based in science, nor in sound medical practice. Fear drove us into isolation and minimal contact with the patients. There was almost no one touching these patients with bare hands — very sad for them and their families, being starved of touch that would have eased their suffering.

The 1918 influenza outbreak, spread in part by the military during World War One, was responsible for over one-hundred-million deaths worldwide. Reportedly, thirty-five-million have succumbed to HIV. And here we are in 2020 and 2021 with COVID-19, and so far millions have died.

Trauma was a scourge for me. Room Ten, talk about a nightmare. I don't even like to watch gory movies let alone see such gore in person; Room Ten, the trauma room in one of the county hospitals, was a combined emergency room/operating room. During my rotation there I, along with other students, was tasked with recording and observing the trauma for each patient.

During third- and fourth-year clinical rotations we were issued pagers. Those little black pagers were another badge of honor that most of us learned to hate; one intern slammed his into the wall, smashing it after it went "beep-beep-beep" one too many times. Regardless of whether you were sleeping in the call room, eating, or otherwise occupied, a page of "10" meant to head immediately to the trauma room. On the way in, you were handed a clipboard with paper and a pen to write down as much as possible as the trauma team treated the patient. Easy to note the time of each intervention and medication given, but it was really impossible to write everything down in most cases, as the room erupted in controlled chaos, with a dozen members of the trauma team doing a bloody dance of repair and resuscitation.

I hated Room Ten. Trauma is profoundly messier in real life than on popular, medical television series. Imagine the worst bloodiest horror movie you ever watched, then imagine you are in the middle of it in real life. What does it sound like, what does it smell like, what do broken bones and punctured flesh really look like, where is the blood coming from, and how much blood is there? The case I remember most clearly was a young man whose pelvis had been crushed by a large piece of machinery that had fallen on him on the job site. The echoes of his wailing and shrieking reach across the years to make me weep even now. It was clear that he would lose at least a leg and maybe his life. All the while I simply observed, writing down the clinical particulars that in no way captured this man's agony and fear. I was just writing a list. It was horrible since I also could imagine Ian's last moments, even if I didn't want to.

I do not remember anyone comforting this profoundly crushed man. We were all too busy doing our jobs.

Blood has a warm and pungent fragrance, a deep odor like wet earth in early spring. If you have had a bad bloody nose you know it well. Usually the smell of blood, like unexpected helicopters, signals trouble, which may evoke a sense of resignation. Smells trigger feelings, whether we want to admit it or not, whether you can push those thoughts aside or not. That senior who smells of cigarettes, coffee, and shampoo reminds you of your grandmother, and the middle-aged man with the wrong kind of sweat covered with aftershave turns your stomach. Perhaps the patient has a leaky bladder. The homeless smell of poor access to hygiene and the clothes they are wearing. I can still smell the burn unit where I worked during a later rotation; skin on fire brings to mind Silvadine dressings, painful debridements, and more wails of agony. All familiar places have their signature scents: the health food store or the spa, your dentist's office with its sickly clean smell, but the hospital has an aggressive, chemically sterile odor. My clinic smells of alcohol swabs and hand sanitizer. Room Ten was an overload of all the senses, an array of scents and sounds, suffocating trauma, painted with fear and pain.

Another Room Ten case. A man stepped into an elevator and one of the cables broke, leaving him hanging upside down inside the elevator, his leg pinched at the knee between the top of the elevator and the floor, his lower leg on the outside of the elevator. It was after hours and he had told his wife not to call him at work because he was tired of her nagging him. Although worried, she hadn't called. By the time he presented to trauma, half a day later, there was no saving the leg so it was neatly amputated in the OR, leaving a tidy stump.

His wife did not want to visit him on the postoperative ward. She was freaked out by the loss of his leg, maybe feeling guilty she hadn't called, maybe angry he had told her not to. She was sent a Polaroid of the stump to look at in advance of the real thing. I believe she finally visited him on the ward, but I always wanted to know how the rest of that story played out. If Room Ten kept a yearbook it would be filled with horrific snapshots of real lives, without backstory or redemption. Writing details on a clipboard is just like counting bones or listing the objects in your purse or backpack.

Those years of clinical training flood my mind with visuals. The first time I assisted in the operating room for an aortic aneurysm repair. Assisting involves a large amount of time spent holding retractors, usually in the most awkward and biomechanically disadvantageous positions. Were the surgeons or nurses doing that on purpose? As you tire, the surgeon barks at you to hold still or pull harder or move to another impossible position. In that aortic aneurysm case, the surgeon took my gloved hand, guiding it deep into the abdominal cavity through the layers of skin, fat, fascia, and intestine to touch the aorta, deep and warm and pulsing, the largest vessel in the body. I promptly felt faint and had to leave the operating room. I sat on the floor outside the OR until I'd convinced myself I felt better, but as soon as I entered the OR again I felt faint. My body once again failed me, forcing me to leave a second time. I did not go back in. The patient did well initially, but later died; showers of emboli slowly knocked out all his organs. There is only so much even a skilled surgeon or physician can do if the disease is determined to take its victim, another objective hazard of medicine.

I have always been a fainter; I learned quickly during medical school that lack of food, lack of sleep, and unexpectedly having to view major, bloody traumas were triggers. Perhaps I have an over-active, sympathetic nervous system (which is not to say I am overly sympathetic, but that might be true also). So, I tried to anticipate, as much as I could, what might suddenly present itself; I ate a little more for breakfast, or in the evening if I was working overnight on call. Coffee and bananas were my go-to breakfast, quick in the morning, and easy to throw up if I was confronted with massive bleeding or bones sticking out where they shouldn't. I became good at recognizing the pre-symptoms of fainting: sudden sweat and ringing in my ears, and I'd sit with my head down immediately so I wouldn't pass out, a version of stop-drop-and-roll to avoid a faint. If you wait until the tunnel vision comes, it might be too late to avoid unconsciousness.

If you are unconscious, you can't help anyone, including yourself — that's why you put your oxygen mask on first, before assisting others.

PART VI

ORGANS OF VOICE AND RESPIRATION

you cannot speak if you do not breathe

MOUNT RAINIER, ALSO KNOWN AS TAHOMA,
RISING MAJESTICALLY FROM THE FOREST BELOW.

fig. 6–1

THE LARYNX

———

a finite number of words to speak?

I was in clinical rotations in 1991, the year following my Master's degree; Dick was finishing his fourth year, and applying for internships and residency. We still lived in the old house I had purchased at Bayless Place and managed to spend a bit of time together here and there, but we both had ridiculously busy schedules, sometimes going days without seeing each other.

"If you never do anything when you are tired, then you will never do anything at all," Dick always said.

The rare times we did have the same evening or day off, we would go for walks with the dogs or out for breakfast, no matter how sleepy we were. Consider this. There are 168 hours in a week; medical residents reportedly work an average of eighty to one-hundred-dred hours per week on a fixed salary. As an intern, a couple years later, I was making just a little above the minimum wage of $4.25 per hour. There are reports of residents working up to 136 hours in a week. If a resident slept the recommended eight hours per night, that would leave only between an hour and a half and four hours per day to do everything else: including caring for dependents, trying to maintain a relationship, getting gas for the car, showering, getting dressed, buying groceries, cooking, buying toilet paper, and all the other mundane things that ordinary people need to do. Forget cleaning the toilet, or organizing the pantry. Of course, sleeping is not a valued activity in the hospital, and at home many residents will sacrifice sleep in favor of feeding their dog or their children or spending time with their partners.

While I do value the privilege granted me to learn such a large amount in such a short space of time, I can't help but ask at what cost? A 1996 report indicated that residents slept an average of 2.7 hours per day while on call, and more than one report has described increased incidence of car crashes for medical residents driving home following extended in-hospital shifts, often with fatalities. If we as physicians believe that proper sleep, exercise, healthy diet, and stress management are important for optimal health, then why don't we promote those values in our training programs?

The answer, in part, is economics. Residency programs are still a source of cheap labor; the bottom line is most important. This is even more the case now that financial CEOs and CFOs (who may never have practiced medicine) are running the show. Residents are considered by the health care system as full-time equivalents (FTE), their salaries evaluated as equivalent to an MD, even though they work a stupid number of hours. For CEOs and CFOs looking at the financial bottom line, resident physicians are the human cogs in the machine that will save the organization money. Medical students are a real bonus, since they actually pay for the luxury of working for a hospital or health care network.

The culture of abuse in medical training goes back decades, and derives from the idea that one must harden trainees in order for them to perform complex tasks perfectly, like hundreds of diamonds created by extreme pressure to set their so called perfection; meaning they should function without making a mistake, and require little maintenance. Capable and accurate providers will not make waves, but will stand their ground, taking any tsunami without complaint. This culture silences the larynx, frowns upon speaking out. Sadly, as ever, in the COVID-19 pandemic, healthcare workers have suffered along with those who are sick and those who have lost loved ones. It is not sustainable.

Due to long hours, on-call duties, study requirements, mismatched locations, and schedules, Dick and I found our time together eroded. As if we did not have enough work to do, we also had to pass our National Board Exams, a series of standardized tests that ran through medical school and internship, with minutia presented in K-questions, which are designed to confuse even the most well rested minds.

"Which of the following choices may or may not be correct in a particular circumstance?"

This would be followed by the infamous A, B, C, D, multiple choices which are etched into every medical student's mind from that era. An ambiguous question was followed by the alphabetic choices, which then would be parsed further to: option number 1-A only; 2-A and C; 3-B and d; 4-A, B, C; and 5-all of the above. Groaning,

I added these K-questions, and all standardized tests designed to spiral the tired mind into spaghetti, to the juggle of clinical rotations, grief, and love.

As our schedules fell more and more out of sync, Dick spent more time with his friends including Wade, a medical student also from Southern California. Wade was intelligent but profoundly incompetent when dealing with snow and ice. Never mind driving, this SoCal transplant to Minnesota could barely walk across any icy sidewalk without wiping out. People who grow up in the north know how to walk on ice — remember the penguins? Apparently, Wade had no instinct for self-preservation. His first year in Minnesota, he continued to ride his skinny-tyred, ten-speed bike to school deep into winter, well beyond what would be reasonable without studded tires. He crashed on his way to school one icy, December day; his wrecked ten-speed, thin tyres bent like two giant potato chips. It spent the rest of the winter locked to the bike rack and covered in snow. After falling more times in four years of medical school than he had in his entire life, Wade took a residency position in a warmer climate out west.

Dick also had women friends who were younger medical students. I did not judge whom he was spending time with while I was busy with rotations, after all what is a relationship without trust? There was one weekend that he went away to a cabin up north with one of those friends, reportedly with a larger group of medical students, most of whom I did not know. That did give me a pang of doubt.

After my next-to-last year in medical school, Dick graduated and accepted an internship position several states to the east. I stayed in my house at Bayless Place in St. Paul to finish my MD. Internship, the first year of residency, can be a stand-alone year, or in some programs, it is part of the longer residency. His was a pre-liminary year, during which he applied for a surgical, sub-specialty residency. Although we had no specific plans for the future, I had the idea that Dick would come back in a year or more to finish training in Minnesota. Again, the fuzzy plans.

Over the four-and-a-half years we were together, we had a few arguments. At the time, this did not strike me as unusual, but with that pesky hindsight perhaps I should have known all along. Once, we disagreed about whether a canceled cheque could count as a receipt or proof of payment. Paper cheques were routed through the banks to be stamped or canceled to prove they had been paid. They were then mailed back to the original cheque writers. Careful people would then go through the stacks of paper cheques to recon-cile them with the paper bank statements; others just threw them in boxes to store in case they needed to go through them at a later date. I felt sure that a cheque with the bank stamp could be used as proof of payment. Dick insisted I was not correct, that a separate receipt for any particular transaction should be kept. He may have been right, but why were we arguing about such a petty thing?

Another dispute involved the correct way to squeegee the wind-shield of the car at the gas station. The pattern I used to squeegee the glass apparently was not the proper combination of vertical and horizontal, and resulted in insulting streaks. Since Dick had once worked at a gas station and it really wasn't that important to me, I deferred to his greater expertise.

He once said to me, "Imagine you have a finite number of words to use in your lifetime and you have already used up half of them."

I laughed at the time.

Now I know he was not joking. My academic year 1991–92 was spent in final clinical rotations interspersed with trips out east to visit Dick. One rotation was internal medicine, the non-surgical treatment of diseases and disorders that affect the internal organs, including heart, lungs, kidney, liver, stomach, intestines — any organ between your head and your hips. ICU and critical care are in many ways an accounting challenge, ins and outs, IV and pee; a well-known rule of thumb is to be careful not to turn someone into a waterfall, IV fluids pouring in from the top, then a diuretic and a catheter causing it all to flow out into the plastic bag at the bottom. Electrolyte levels must be carefully monitored, along with urine output, blood pressure, and drug levels. Daily lab results were reviewed, and adjustments made as necessary, turning patients into a chemistry experiment in real time, reminiscent of a marathon.

Rounds on the internal medicine ward always reminded me of a momma duck with her ducklings. The attending physician led the pack, or, if absent, then the senior resident could lead, proudly strutting his or her long coat and stethoscope. The language of the stethoscope shouted out the wearer's specialty, with internists wearing the instrument around their necks, sub-specialties like general surgery coiling it in the pocket of their white coats, and psychiatrists (and ophthalmologists) generally keeping it in a desk drawer. Like other flashy accessories, the most expensive stethoscopes do not always correlate with the expertise of the owner.

The lead physician was trailed by one to three junior residents or interns, who also wore long coats, but looked more disheveled and more harried. At the end of the flock would be one to four medical students in short white coats with stethoscopes self-consciously draped over their necks or nervously tucked into a pocket. A couple of us once in a while quietly quacked as we trailed along at the back of the pack. Possibly, that was just me quacking.

The suspense of new rotations was that you might be aggressively ignored or, alternatively, randomly put on the spot in front of the other team members, the patient, nurses, and any visitors or family members at the bedside. Mostly the senior residents or physician would ignore you and then suddenly launch a question when you least expected it. Just as your eyelids were sinking shut, they'd throw a ninja star in the form of a question like, "What is the significance of an S1 S2 split on auscultation?" which is a cardiac question, but posed in the case of a patient with gastrointestinal problems.

Senior residents or attending physicians seemed to have radar to detect the weakest, most-fatigued member of the team, and they'd instantly find the least answerable question in order to optimize the on-the-spot training, a process similar to the alpha wolf culling the weaker members of the pack. This meant each of us carried a fight-or-flight anxiety on top of our dead-tiredness, and made our daily existence about as comfortable as lying on a cold concrete sidewalk, on stale cigarette butts, in downtown Minneapolis on the coldest November day.

That year, I applied for residency placements, choosing a more competitive specialty, ophthalmology, and sent applications to a number of programs around the country. Ophthalmology — my specialty — is a nice blend of surgery and internal medicine, without the heartbreak of major trauma in most cases. From time to time, depending on one's sub-specialty, ophthalmologists are faced with significant facial injuries in the context of accidents, but for most clinic-based, general, eye MDs this will not be your daily duty. Ophthalmology holds some glacial heartbreaks, like a patient losing her sight from relentless glaucoma over years, or even months, but there are also huge opportunities to prevent blindness and treat vision loss. Even for those who lose vision, support can be offered, and people with profound loss of sight can live full lives.

I was fortunate to get interviews around the country that added traveling for interviews to my busy schedule, while I was still trying to squeeze in a few visits to see Dick out east. I had two interviews in New York City in the fall. I had been to Manhattan more than once as a tourist, but you look at a place with different eyes if you imagine you might be living there. New York City was gray, dirty, oppressively concrete, with endless traffic blaring horns for no apparent reason. Without a single green leaf or blade of grass, it felt like Batman's Gotham City. The time of year didn't help, turning an exciting trip to the big city into an airless, depressing visit. One interview was at a public hospital. The residents all looked like they had been run over by a bus, which seemed strange since ophthalmology is typically one of the gentler sub-specialties, in contrast to something like general surgery.

"So tell me about the program," I asked the students.

Their glazed eyes darted away before they answered in overly vague terms. Then came the piece of information that made me decide this was not the program for me. I was told it was perfectly safe to exit the medical complex by one door, but that the other exit, just a block away, led onto a street where it was unsafe to walk unescorted, day or night.

The second interview in New York City was at a very reputable eye hospital in an upscale area. In a posh, spacious boardroom, my place was indicated, and I sat expectantly on the chair at the head of the long, wooden table. I faced six, well-groomed physician interviewers who sat, three on each side, in their spick-and-span, long, white coats, worn over their dress shirts. On the table were what looked like little metal monopoly playing pieces: the dog, the shoe, the wheelbarrow. Were they a distraction, a psychological decoy to derail the interviewee? Puzzled why they were there, I said nothing, and just swept them aside with the back of my hand.

"Dr. Anderson, do you agree with Dr. Kevorkian?" was the opening question.

Kevorkian was an advocate for physician-assisted dying long before it was considered a reasonable end-of-life option. At that time, assisting death was criminal. Like Goldilocks, after tasting these two options, I left New York City, and went in search of a placement elsewhere, hoping for a residency program that was neither a crime scene, nor full of mind games.

Another interview was in New Orleans. This program involved a number of hospitals that residents rotated through, much like the two New York City programs rolled into one. At the first one, a private hospital, a dedicated security guard escorted one from the hushed, plush-carpeted hallways to the parkade. The second one, where I underwent a further interview, was at the other end of the spectrum — the eye clinic at the New Orleans Charity Hospital, which did not have enough chairs so people spilled out of the waiting room to sit on the floor in the hallway. "The Big Free," as it was called, Charity Hospital was even more Gotham than New York City. It loomed into the sky, its concrete walls stained with water-streaks and despair. It remained abandoned for years in the aftermath of hurricane Katrina, and was later demolished.

Late one night, sometime in amongst the rotations, long hours, and interviews, I was watching television after a thousand-hour shift. (Sleepless shifts always felt eternal even if they were just twenty-four to thirty hours.) One ad stood out among the other more ordinary commercials. The announcement told me to mail a postcard to enter a lottery to buy tickets to the 1991 World Series, the greatest World Series of all time. The Minnesota Twins had made it to the series that year, and if one wasn't already a season ticket holder there was a lottery to buy four tickets for the entire set of games. Through the fog of fatigue, I obeyed the television, dutifully copied the address onto a postcard to request the chance to buy tickets to the World Series.

As luck would have it, I won and I bought the tickets. Kirby Puckett was a star Twins player that season. He later retired as a result of vision loss due to a retinal vein occlusion and glaucoma. I had the chance to meet Kirby Puckett in person years later at the Academy of Ophthalmology annual meeting in Chicago. He had become a spokesman for a pharmaceutical company that made glaucoma drops. We shook hands briefly. Puckett was about Ian's height, only a few inches taller than I am, but he was fifty pounds heavier, solid as cement, and very friendly in that short encounter.

With one set of World Series tickets, Dick and I took my ten-year-old nephew and my elderly neighbor Ted to game two. The Metrodome Stadium in Minneapolis, which has since been replaced, was a pressurized building with a muffin-like white canvas roof held up by the denser air inside, differential pressure whooshing through as you entered the doors. Ted was barely larger than my nephew and I remember holding both of their hands so they wouldn't be blown down as we went in and out of the dome. My nephew still remembers how loud it was and the sea of white "homer-hankies" that waved all around the venue. Everyone yelled, "K-i-i-i-i-r-by Puckett!" each time he came to bat or made a defensive play. The series was going on right in the middle of my residency interviews, so I had to give away the other tickets to my siblings. The Twins won the series at home October 27, 1991, which I heard about while on an airplane back from New York City. My older sister Jeanne had the luck of being there for the series-winning home game.

I still remember pushing the large envelope with my application for ophthalmology residency at the Mayo Clinic into the mail slot and hoping for the best. I wanted to stay in Minnesota partly because my friends and family were there, but I also believed Dick might return for training after his internship year away.

I was very pleased to get notification of an interview at the clinic in Rochester, not only because it fit my criteria of staying in the state, but because it also fulfilled a childhood dream. The Mayo Clinic was and still is considered the epitome of medical care. It was founded by the Mayo brothers, Charles and William, after a tornado had devastated the area, causing widespread injuries. The brothers partnered with the local convent to provide care, which led to the creation of Saint Mary's hospital. The Mayo brothers were visionaries with an inspired view of medical care and a long view to the future. They even bought significantly more materials than needed for one of their first buildings, the Mayo building, in order to be able to expand it in the future. These materials were, in fact, used decades later. The rectangular pattern of gray tones and white marble tiles reaching up the side of the building, where I spent most of my ophthalmology residency, is stuck permanently in my visual memories.

My family had a personal connection with the Mayo Clinic. My great-aunt Bessie had been a medical secretary there early in the twentieth century, which was a bragging point for my mom.

As a grade-school student, I went on a field trip to see the place. I remember two things, first there were many tall buildings and second there was an exhibit of objects people had swallowed that had been removed by surgery. It was an impressive display of oddities, including a large safety pin and various other metal objects.

My interview for an ophthalmology residency at the Mayo Clinic took place in October, 1991, just a few days after the Minnesota Twins won the World Series. While waiting for my interview, I met another prospective candidate, from New York City. He confided to me that he was terrified to see the acres of cornfields and trees surrounding the town of Rochester. I told him I had been just as terrified to see the endless concrete and barren landscape of Manhattan. I was on familiar ground in the middle of that pastoral environment and felt right at home. The interviews went smoothly, but at the end of the day the world turned into a snow globe. More than three feet of snow fell before the storm was over. I'm sure that was the last straw for the candidate from New York City.

That Halloween Blizzard of 1991 was epic, dropping almost thirty-seven inches of snow and responsible for the death of twenty-two people. My old neighbor Ted later told me the event was on par with the Armistice Day Blizzard of 1940 that he had lived through. That blizzard dropped only twenty-seven inches of snow, he said, and heavy winds resulted in a death toll of 145.

I am not sure whether I was just anxious to get home, underestimated the amount of snow, or over-estimated my driving skills and the ability of the highway crews to clear the highway, but I decided to drive home the next day. Heavy blizzards shroud everything in a thick layer of snow, producing an undulating contour like the mounds of mashed potatoes at Thanksgiving dinners. Shapes only hint at the lawnmower someone did not have time to rescue before the storm, or the patio chairs still waiting for that last, nice fall day. Sounds are dampened, and all objects, including parked cars, disappear into shades of white, with the roads and sidewalks all deserted. The only good thing about driving under those conditions is that if you end up in the ditch, provided you don't hit another car on the way, it is a soft landing. In rural areas, it is a leap of faith to set off on a road trip on a day like that. You might be an hour or more into your drive before you determine that it's not a good idea to be on the road; and by that time there might be nowhere to stop since it's probably many miles between gas stations, towns, or rest stops. It's usually a bad idea to stop on the side of the road as you're likely to be rear-ended. I was lucky. I made it to my house after a very long day of white-knuckle driving, plowing my car into the heavy drift in the driveway in order to be off the street.

"Happy Halloween," I told myself, relieved I'd made it home.

THE DANGER IS MORE APPARENT FROM ABOVE THAN FROM THE
PERSPECTIVE OF THE CLIMBERS TRAVERSING THE GLACIER.

fig. 6–2

FALSE VOCAL CORDS

---

things are not always what they seem

While I was waiting to begin my residency at the Mayo Clinic, Dick was still interning. Each journey to visit him involved a commercial flight, followed by a drive of about two hours in a rental car along country roads. I listened to a lot of music CDs on my way to and from the airport. Dick had leased a classic two-storey, stained wood house perched on the edge of a large lot, where he lived with Mike the dog.

Mike continued to be crazy as usual. On one of my visits, he leapt through the screen of a second-storey window to cruise the neighborhood for a few days before we finally found him. Later that winter, while we were out for a walk, Mike bolted off a cliff at the edge of a frozen, snow covered lake. Thankfully, he fell only about fifteen feet into two feet of powder, which buffered his fall, a soft landing. We went for walks in the forest and spent time on the river nearby. The hills around this house featured towering forests with hidden trails to explore.

Once, when the telephone rang at the house, I answered since Dick was not home (every other night he was on call), but there was only hollow silence on the line. I asked him about it later.

"Who knows. Just forget about it," he replied. "Stop being so paranoid."

I did not forget, and asked myself why he would think I was being paranoid? I was growing uneasy about our relationship. Dick had his women friends who were medical students, and while I told myself to be open minded and trusting, I was having doubts about those friendships. Had he spent that weekend at the cabin with a group of medical students, or had he really been with one of his woman friends?

My large family always accommodated Dick, and grumbled only occasionally about his demeanor, which could be dismissive and abrasive. And the stupid arguments between us kept flaring. How to properly wash the windshield, had I already used half of my life's allotment of words? — in other words, "Shut up!"

It seems I was blinded by my wish to be part of a duo, my fear of being solo, and my idea that if I tried hard enough, I could conquer anything. Ian's words came back to sting me. "What if you're just in love with the idea of being in love?" I had almost always been able to accomplish what I set my mind to, if I worked hard enough and long enough. Everything except for my relationship with Ian, cut short by his death. The adage "if at first you don't succeed, try and try again" must have been tattooed on my soul by the greater fates, or maybe by my parents' encouragement. Where is that balance between giving up too easily and putting too much of your blood in the game? At some point pursuit of the goal may kill you, which is a literal risk in mountain climbing and a metaphoric risk in romantic love, which can certainly feel like dying. Perhaps a better strategy for life than blindly slogging ahead is: Step. Rest. Step. Rest. Reconsider. Make a good choice before repeating, repeating, repeating.

Sometime in the months that followed the mysterious telephone call, Dick finally came clean by telling me he had met another woman. Her father had just died, which set me thinking maybe he had been attracted to me in the first place because he saw my brokenness. Anyway, a damsel in distress almost always regains her composure. Dick's stated reason for our break-up was that I was "rough around the edges" and already "married to that dead guy." His evidence was the ring I'd had made with the money from Ian's bank account and that I still owned.

Ian and Ian's death are like two different people. One I loved in a present moment that is now past, the other is a final and finite character branded on my heart. The first has no future, the second requires attention. That scar of remembering the departed beloved is to be cherished as you make a future without them. Forgetting the dead is not a prerequisite for moving forward. You can and must keep your loved one in your heart, even if they have died; it only makes sense really, there are people who have had an important effect on your life and their death doesn't erase their life or their effect on you. So in reality, these beloved are dead, but most definitely not gone. A fact Dick did not understand. Also a fact that, in 2020, CNN reporter Wolf Blitzer repeated nightly to those who lost loved ones to COVID-19, "May their memories be a blessing." I do love this saying because memories of loved ones are a blessing.

Once Dick and I broke up, in the fall of 1991, he wanted all his things back. He had left a lot at my house in St Paul. He even wanted the pie-safe and the bed he had made. The latter was really just two-by-four wooden studs and plywood, worth less than ten dollars. It was the most crudely constructed piece of furniture he had made — perhaps I should have noticed the comparative lack of attention he gave to the building of our bed than to the other furniture he made. He wanted it back nonetheless, and I arranged to give it to him because I didn't want it, and giving it back was the right thing to do, although I would have preferred to destroy it in a blazing firepit. While destruction may give temporary satisfaction, a wise woman once told me, you only know you are truly free when you are indifferent. I did not burn or destroy anything. Nor did I regret the dividing up of goods between us. We set a day in spring for him to come to the house to get his things. I asked my parents to come over for moral support.

"Do you want me to punch him out?" my dad asked.

Kind of sweet and weird at the same time, since as far as I knew my dad had never punched anyone. Anyway, I had seen more than enough trauma at that point in my life and had no wish to see more.

"No," I said. "Just be nice and polite. That will make him more uncomfortable."

The day came. Both my parents were sitting on the couch, and I was in the kitchen. Dick walked through the front door, saw my parents, looked away, and hustled off like a rodent to gather his things. He had traded in his Volkswagen Westphalia van and the Scout, and loaded everything into a shiny, new, big, black pickup truck. He was playing the macho surgeon-to-be. After several trips from the house to the truck, he approached me in the backyard, well away from the living room, where my parents were still patiently sitting on the couch.

"Why are your parents here?

"They are here to support me," I said calmly.

He just seemed confused by that, perhaps surprised I wasn't dissolving into histrionics like the heroines of old black-and-white movies. Perhaps he wanted me to beg him not to leave. My parents steadfastly stayed in the living room a couple hours or more, making small talk each time Dick walked through with his things. They acted just as I had requested, unfailingly nice and polite the whole time. It was supremely awkward. I could tell Dick had no idea what to make of it.

Months of second-guessing followed that spring. Why had I consistently given Dick the benefit of the doubt and accepted his judgment that I was being paranoid, while he'd been lying to me the whole time? To be fair to myself, I had never really believed I was being paranoid, I just hadn't had any real proof otherwise. This leads to the next question, which is why did I put up with his treatment of me if I did not trust him? Like a branch floating down a stream, each inquiry leads to another. Why didn't I listen to my family's grumbles? Why did I let things float so far downstream? Which leads to more questions and possible excuses and reasoning and finally just ties your psyche into knots. Losing a love to untruth and betrayal is a loss. This almost felt worse, since it was a leaving with agency, it was Dick's choice. But hurt is hurt and it does not matter which is worse. Another wound. Once again, my heart was heavy. Although not as shocking as the avalanche, this split was a messy mudslide of emotions. Why I tried to salvage the relationship is a mystery to me, but I guess I shouldn't blame myself for his lying and cheating; another wise woman told me later that I should be kind to my younger self. Had I been Aurora, I would have turned him into a thirteen-lined ground squirrel and watched him scurry off.

On one hand I was successful—MD/MS degrees, home-owner, an intern at the Hennepin County Medical Centre in Minneapolis, accepted to the Mayo Clinic ophthalmology residency—on the other hand I was solo again.

I was not that successful woman the Enjoli perfume television commercial purred about, who could, "bring home the bacon, fry it up in a pan, and never let you forget you're a man." I could bring home the bacon and fry it up in a pan for sure, but the other stuff not so much. In June, 1986, *Newsweek* reported that women of a certain age were more likely to get killed by a terrorist than to get married. Now I felt like Dickens's Miss Havisham, waiting for her groom who never shows. I had been thrown into the garbage, like a piece of leftover trash, no more valued than the crumpled scrap of paper on which you scrawl your last grocery list—dog food, toilet paper, me. Apparently, this is why people use the word "dumped".

What about the "rough around the edges" comment? This was just like my mother's "you walk too athletically" remark. So what, and too bad. There is nothing to fix. So what if I am too short, or not pretty enough, and have a bumpy nose. Some criticize my whimsical ways, others complain I am too careful. What can be done about any of that? Love me, or don't love me, but don't try to whittle me down due to your own insecurities; strength is a gift, not a challenge. So there I was, a successful failure. But I was not ready to abandon the idea of someday having a life partner and raising a family.

On my thirtieth birthday, in 1992, I graduated from medical school on the heels of being dumped. What symmetry. College had been all about my Bachelor's degree, and Ian, and getting into medical school; medical school had been all about finishing my MS and MD, and Dick, and getting into residency. Nice packages of five to six years punctuated by one actual death and one relationship death. It was time once again to reinvent myself. I was just like the Timex watch, taking a licking and keeping on ticking.

Thirty years old felt super old. Tick tock. Along with my fundamental plan to be a doctor, I always imagined myself married with children. At this rate, I might have one of the two. It was hard at first to give up on Dick, even though he was a liar, a cheat, and, frankly, mean, since it meant losing half my dream. In many ways the loss of the relationship was not about him; I could see half my future disappearing into thin air. This time I did not fight with Mabel over the loss, but I did feel her presence again, keenly.

Newly single, I began my internship at the local county hospital in June, 1992, once again putting my head down to march on. If medical school is like drinking from a fire hose in terms of knowledge and content, internship is like being thrown over Niagara Falls without a barrel.

MY MOM AND DAD, KATHERINE (KAY) AND JAMES (JIM) ANDERSON,
HAVE HAD MY BACK FOR MY ENTIRE LIFE, EVEN IF THEY DID
NOT ALWAYS UNDERSTAND OR APPROVE OF WHAT I WAS DOING.
MARRIED 70 YEARS SO FAR IN THIS PICTURE, CHRISTMAS 2022.

fig. 6–3

TRUE VOCAL CORDS

---

when you find truth, you find strength

Months turned into years, I fell again, picked myself up, and put myself together again. Each fall was painful, but putting myself back together got easier. I didn't waste time pushing back, I just wallowed in the pit until I was ready to climb out again. Tuck and roll was (and still is) my mantra, just as when you're running on ice and you fall — tuck and roll — then, when you're ready, stand up again. I knew that the pit was not infinite and when the time came, I would put my head up and dust myself off.

I finished my internship at the county hospital in Minneapolis and then my residency in ophthalmology at the Mayo Clinic. All the experiences I have had, and all the people I've met, sometimes make me feel like Walter Mitty, except it was not just all in my imagination. I earned a private pilot's license during my residency, and on one memorable landing I informed the tower of the small airport, "There's a kitty on the runway." There was in fact a kitten and, thankfully, I was able to steer the small Cessna 150 around the poor animal, that then departed the runway under its own power. For a time, while training at the Mayo Clinic, I moonlighted as the night doctor in a medium-security, federal prison, which involved wearing a large utility belt with keys on a big chain and a walkie-talkie that would sound an alarm if dropped. Each time I went to work, I passed through a series of electronic gates and guarded doors that reminded me of the television series *Get Smart* from my childhood.

After a decade of training, I completed my ophthalmology residency. I did find what I thought was love and married eventually, which prompted my move to Calgary, Alberta, in 1997. That same year, I did my final fellowship year of training under the mentorship of Doctor Howard Gimbel, who was a pioneer in cataract and refractive surgery, and who is still my friend. It turns out the excimer laser discovery was to have a big impact on my career in refractive surgery.

Besides becoming a high-volume, woman surgeon building my own medical practice, I also managed to find my inner artist, sculpting in clay, bronze, plaster, felt, steel, and butter. Over my years working at the Gimbel Eye Centre, I published textbooks and articles in my field, and, outside of work, I travelled, volunteered in grade schools, and at bingo fundraisers. I was declared "Officially Amazing" as a member of that *Guinness Book of World Records* longest indoor soccer game — and have a certificate to prove it. Of course, I continued to write, take baths, buy flowers, and have dogs.

Ian and the avalanche became more distant, as would be expected, although from time to time I still corresponded with his parents, and Carleton College set up an award in his name, so he was not forgotten. The Ian Kraabel Memorial Prize/History is described this way: "Established in 1987 by the classmates and friends of Ian Kraabel '85, who died in an avalanche on Mount Baker in the summer of 1986, this award honors Ian's unusual intensity, originality, and athletic ability. The Ian Kraabel Memorial Prize in History is awarded each year by the Department of History to the Senior History major who best reflects Ian's personal qualities and his desire to pursue understanding and knowledge." To date there have been thirty-five recipients.

"You were a lot nicer after Ian died," my mother remarked one day years later when his name had come up in conversation.

"I suppose you're right," I agreed, although I didn't feel I had been awful before the accident, perhaps just overconfident. "It helped me become more empathetic and understanding."

"Definitely nicer," Mom confirmed with a smile.

Although I no longer thought about Ian and the avalanche daily, as a result of my experiences, a splinter of fear that loved ones in my life might suddenly disappear had worried itself into my soul. That splinter was with me when I entered a corral to try to catch a horse in among about twenty other horses as part of a beginner's western horsemanship class. I was a novice horse-handler boldly wading right into the middle of thousands of pounds of horses milling around in the muddy paddock. Snorts and warm, coarse-haired, horse bellies crushing in, manure mingling in the stirred-up soil, horses bumping up against one another, nipping, a few skittering sideways, bolting to the side, their backs at the level of my face.

I put my hands up to their sides and gave a calm, firm push to avoid being knocked down.

At that moment, I was sharply aware that I was unafraid. It was an equine-inspired epiphany. I was not afraid. For so many years of my life people around me had remarked I was too nervous and should just relax if I said things like, "Stay away from the edge of that cliff; don't stand under it because a rock might fall on your head; look both ways before crossing the street; and do not go hiking alone." After all it is prudent to avoid objective hazards. I was always watching for the potential for injury in any situation.

"Don't let fear stop you from doing things," was a frequent remark, especially as the extreme sports fad took hold. "Stop worrying so much."

Jostled in the middle of all that moving horse flesh, I knew that given my lack of experience, the situation had significant potential for injury for me. I remembered my broken hip and nose from the horse injury when I was a teen. Suddenly I saw that all my fear had been fear for other people's safety. I was not afraid for myself at all. If a bear rips off your ear, then you will fear bears or possibly all large carnivores. After I did a 360-degree spin on black ice in rush hour traffic in my 1968 Bronco, I feared driving on icy roads for a long time. For the primitive part of my brain, the amygdala, the world in general had been proven to be a dangerous place for people I loved; all that fear I carried within me was fear that other people's well-being was in danger. All the while I'd cultivated the Teflon exterior that medical training encourages and cared for sick and injured patients — daily proof that the world is a dangerous place. Dick had always made it across the street regardless of my worry. Recognizing the truth that I was not afraid for myself was a big step in managing my fear for other people's safety.

Over the years, I've helped to care for people injured in car accidents, in falls from roofs and ladders, struck by lightning, electrocuted by power lines, felled by automatic weapons, all things that may or may not have been avoidable. So, in the real world if you can avoid the objective hazard or potential, then you're not going to have to call an ambulance.

Also in the real world, sometimes I'm it; I am the MD when a stranger bites the dust. If I'm the only medically trained person in attendance, then I am expected to deal with it. As the saying goes, it is better to build a fence at the top of a cliff than to park an ambulance at the bottom. I am always looking for the fences. And, as Ted pointed out, if you don't kill yourself in an accident as a young person, then you have a better chance of living a long life.

This realization — that I was not afraid for my own safety — felt like a last bit of healing. I finally had the words to describe my true feelings, and understanding my fear banished that splinter from my soul.

PART VII

ORGANS OF SPECIAL SENSE

the eyes of the soul give the clearest vision

ELLEN AND THE FUTURE REVEREND JENNY CRANE
ON THE PORCH AT SUNWOOD.

fig. 7–1

TRUE SKIN

———————

it's what's underneath that counts

By 2014, I was well settled into my career as an ophthalmologist, having left the Gimbel Eye Centre to establish my own general ophthalmology clinic in Calgary. I was enjoying life with my daughters and my co-workers. As an entrepreneur and mother, I was fully engaged in the rhythm of my day-to-day tasks that ranged from seeing patients, to managing employees, to working on the building we eventually bought to house the clinic, to running my daughters to school or helping with homework.

My days were like ocean waves and tides wafting me up and down a single hallway, dipping me into rooms to examine patients, washing me out again and up to reception to gather another patient to tow back for the next examination. There was an imaginary groove worn in the commercial grade, faux-wood, vinyl floor like a deer trail in the woods. On a good day, the ebb and flow was gentle, punctuated by lunch break and at least one challenging diagnosis.

General ophthalmology, the MD specialty of medical and surgical eye care, is conducted in a dim room reminiscent of a confessional. Every clinic day is larger than life thanks to magnifying lenses and a specialized microscope called a slit lamp that reveals the details of individual eyes, every beautiful, fluted, blue, hazel, gray, or brown iris leading through a smoky or clear lens to the retinal expanses of the back of the eye. Each eye is a secret room revealing clues to the diagnosis. Older patients are pleased to hear, "Your eyes are in great health, see you next year." I am pleased to find treatable conditions to restore vision or prevent blindness.

"The risk is less than one in one-thousand, but are you prepared if you are the *one* who has a bad outcome or complication?" I say to all patients considering elective surgery, and the mountains are still in my mind at those moments.

On a bad day, emergencies or patients who need extra time create log jams, and annoy those waiting for appointments, annihilating any hope of a lunch break. The aftermath is endless apologies without giving away any specifics about the case that threw it all off track. Specific patient details cannot be shared out of respect for each patient, and disclosure of information is forbidden anyway due to privacy rules. *Mea culpa mea culpa mea maxima culpa.* Walk faster between rooms, set aside all but essential tasks with a smile, eventually catch the receding tide by day's end.

As we enter, I motion my patient to the examination chair, the biggest chair in the room, motorized to move up and down, with wipeable, gray upholstery, calling it the "big chair" to steer her away from my five-wheeled stool which once squirted out from under a patient like a watermelon seed and sending her tumbling to the floor. With the heavy, wooden, exam door closed, light from the small desk lamp and the slightly larger corner lamp softly spills into the dark room. At my desk, my fingers hover above the keyboard, ready to enter details into the electronic medical record. The quiet darkness draws out sorrows, a spouse who died recently, a child, the patient faces a terminal diagnosis. My grief has taught me well, and I try to hold space for those whom I see are suffering from loss and fear.

"I am crying all the time—will it damage my eyes?"

"Tears are good for your eyes," and in my mind adding, tears are also good for your soul—no one ever died from crying. If you stop crying you're in deeper trouble. One patient shared that she was in the middle of a trial for the murder of both her parents. Another looked up from his cell phone as I entered the room to whisper, "My sister just died."

A litany of loss—eating disorders in children, cancer, floods, fires, loss of life and home. I am not in the role I imagined I would play as an ophthalmologist. My patients have taught me that there are people attached to those eyes. I carefully place my hand on an arm, the most accepted touch between provider and patient.

"I am so sorry for your loss," I say quietly, along with more practical tips and reassurances, such as: "Tearing does not lead to blindness, it is best to dab your eyes with a cotton handkerchief since the wood fibers in tissues are hard on the skin (and they can scratch your glasses), and a gentle warm compress followed by bland skin cream or ointment will protect your eye lids." There are days filled with humour and whimsy.

"There is a fish in my eye," one man replied upon being asked for his main concern on that visit. Another said, "It looks like there is an engagement ring with a big diamond floating in my vision." "I see a moving dragonfly," was the concern of an older male patient.

The creativity of my patients' ability to categorize their vision symptoms amazes me. Recently swimmers, Mickey Mouse, and a banana have made appearances. These varied objects are conjured from the clear jelly in the back of the eye liquifying over time until it suddenly collapses in on itself like a grape turning into a raisin, a normal part of aging. For the patient it is like looking through a fishbowl in which clumps of clear gelatin intermix and take on shapes. I have seen that fish, the flying dragonfly, and the diamond ring deep in patients' eyes.

"I see blood cells leaking inside my eye," a man announced one day.

I was doubtful, but it turned out that he did have a slow leak from a retinal vessel. The years have taught me to listen to patients, no matter how unusual their descriptions, to try to understand the words they choose to paint the pictures they see. Recently a woman said the exact same thing and it turned out she was correct too.

"I see you've read the medical textbook," I tell patients that come in with a classic description of migraine auras or other common conditions. People offer sketches in pen or pencil of their vision symptoms, particularly those who report auras with or without headaches. At other times it can be very challenging to tease out symptoms, and it's like I've travelled back to those early days of learning the medical interview.

"What kind of problem are you having today?" I ask.

"My vision is blurry," the patient replies.

"Is it one eye or both? How long has it been a problem? Is it for things near or far, and is there anything that makes it better or worse?" I try to hone in on the specifics.

"It's blurry." Or, "It hurts." Or, "Something isn't right." For unclear reasons some individuals simply repeat the same short phrase over and over regardless of the questions. Needless to say, the inability of patients to find the right words to describe their symptoms adds to the challenge of diagnosis and treatment.

A surprising array of things get into people's eyes. Fingernails, thumbs, thumb-tacks, cat claws, dog paws, fish hooks, hairbrushes, mascara brushes, superglue, red ink, knives, forks, paper, ear drops, sticks, thorns from a rose bush, rocks, wires, badminton birdies, soccer balls, horse hooves, pecans, broom handles, flotsam including random fibers, bits of plastic, unidentified mucous-covered particles. One man stepped on the brush end of a push-broom that was lying on the floor and, just like in a cartoon, the handle flew up to smack him in the eye, which resulted in serious injury. Every object in the world has the potential to injure, so it seems absolutely clear to me that everyone should wear safety glasses all the time; more practical advice is to wear safety glasses when recommended, such as in high-risk sports, using power tools, weed-whackers, and other outdoor implements. I spend my days treating common conditions, on the look-out for rare diagnoses that can blind you or kill you. Rare conditions are "zebras" because most of the time it's a horse.

A bonus and blessing in ophthalmology is that I often have the chance to improve vision through treatments such as laser vision correction — made possible by the discovery of the excimer laser's effect on thanksgiving turkey — and cataract surgery. These are the "wow" cases, but I've found there is a softer, equally satisfying "wow" in caring for people who live with low vision and chronic disease, by supporting and saving their remaining vision. Patients with vision impairment navigate the hallway without complaint, one hand trailing along the wall, thanking me for anything that keeps their vision stable. Very old people, over age 90 and a few over 100, shuffle and roll in with walkers, canes, and wheelchairs, mostly with others following in their wake, including in-laws, sons and daughters, nieces, neighbors and friends, who take notes and provide transportation. A few of the extremely-old still ride the bus, and navigate transfers across the city. Like gauze in the wind, the super-old wave off help with a skeletal hand barely covered with translucent skin, only infrequently accepting an arm to travel at a glacial pace from reception to exam room, each step a study in concentration, balance, and will-power.

"How are you doing, Doctor Penno?" is often the first question from super-old or visually impaired patients.

Aroma of hand sanitizer, soap, and alcohol swabs followed me home each evening, the smells of the day, mostly good days, rolling from Monday to Friday in a predicable rhythm. Each day was a series of vignettes, a daily collection of short stories, often repetitive, but sometimes with a twist, offered by patients in the dusk of the examination room. Like rock and mountain climbing, the tasks of a clinic day are engaging and challenging, each with its own reward. And like climbing, when I was in my flow the rest of the world, including the future and past, disappeared. An ophthalmologist is a minister of eyes; the work is looking, listening, sometimes offering real help, sometimes supportive care, pockets of unexpected findings and humanity that paint each clinic day a different hue.

At this point in my life and career I was on an even keel. Having made friends with fear and grief, I could handle the bumps. As a mom, physician, and business owner, I faced each day with purpose. I no longer looked in the mirror and wondered who I was. I no longer wanted to change my name or change my appearance to match my feelings. My true skin matched my outer skin again, including my inner and outer scars; like the dermis that is the true skin nourishes the surface epidermis, my outer self was nourished by my inner self. It felt good to be myself again — wrinkles, gray hairs, and all.

THE TRUSTY WHITE HELMET THAT SAVED ME FROM BEING
INJURED WHEN A FELLOW CLIMBER LOST HIS FOOTING
AND SENT HIS ICE AXE FLYING ONTO MY HEAD.

fig. 7–2

THE LABYRINTH

---

equilibrium is a superpower

Towards the end of one anonymous, mid-week afternoon late in the winter of 2015, I walked a patient back along the plastic planks of the faux, woodgrain floor. After saying goodbye, I circled the waiting room, followed my usual routine, and picked up any stray, balled-up tissues that had escaped patients' hands, each Kleenex tucked into the crevice of a seat cushion reminding me of Jenny. I glanced at the sidewalk through the glass doors to make sure that ice or snow hadn't accumulated while I was in the dark examination room. The clinic schedule was like the gentle waves of a calm ocean, moving me to and fro, according to its own rhythm. I strolled up to reception to grab the next chart, and my receptionist handed me a pink paper message slip.

"A reporter from Seattle called and would like you to call her back," she said.

"Thanks," I said, reading question marks in her pupils, wearing my best blank face, hoping my voice wasn't quivering. I pretended to check out the front windows again for snow and ice.

I knew this was a message about Mount Baker, but did not understand why, after almost thirty years, a reporter would be calling. So many times my thoughts had travelled to retrace the events of the avalanche, and the days leading up to it, that my mind flew through every detail to the inevitable finish, like water flowing down the creek behind my childhood home, each twist and dip leaving as deep a groove in my psyche as that path from exam room to reception. This simple scrap of paper raised other memories, details still buried in cardboard boxes in the back of my closet, sealed with clear packing tape yellowed and cracked from the years and moves between several states and then to Calgary. After a while, drama and trauma had given way to the practicalities of life, as they must. The boxes were there, the memories existed, the events happened, the past cannot be changed, but that does not stop grief from trying to surface. The truce is to package it all up for a later day; that truce was now threatened. I worried about how this resurfacing might affect me, but I knew I must face it.

I casually folded the slip in half, then stuffed it into the front pocket of my black dress pants, the thin message crinkling with each step, distracting me from my next patient. The tiny front fashion pockets of my trousers pushed the sharp edge into the skin above my waistband with each step, like a miniature dog scratching at the door to get out into the yard. Irritated, I repeatedly shoved it back down. Back and forth, up and down the hallway. The last few hours of the day suddenly slowed, the second hand of my watch painfully dragging out each examination, each remaining minute.

Finally, alone at home in my kitchen, I fished out the wrinkled message, smoothing the thin, pink paper on the cool, black slate counter. I took a breath. The sun, nearly set, cast shadows from the poplar trees to the west, creating that same dim lighting as in my exam rooms. With short northern days combined with my occupation, I live my winter life in twilight. Twilight and I are usually friends, the waning light a signal to wind down and reset for the day to come. At that moment the small forest outside my kitchen window, bare trees in the foothills of the Canadian Rockies, usually such a restful scene, was transformed by the fading winter light into a collection of shadows. The trees looked like broken bones.

Next to the little black box check-marked "message" on the designated line on that slip was written, "Allison Williams, reporter. *Seattle Met Magazine.*" Twenty-eight years and six months had passed. There she was again, Mabel. The familiar cascade of deep sorrow washed over me. Another rogue wave that took my breath away.

I picked up the telephone and studied the number. After another pause, another breath, I called Allison Williams. Allison told me she was working on an article for an upcoming issue of the *Seattle Metropolitan Magazine.*

"Are you the Ellen Anderson who was on Mount Baker in 1986 when an avalanche killed Ian Kraabel?" she asked.

"Why now?" I quizzed, feeling angry that a stranger would drag me to the past. Memories continued to flood back with echoing sadness. Another deep breath, a sigh. Finally, I could not stop my tears.

During the summer of 2014, the glacier had spit out a backpack. Typical of a glacier, extremely slow moving except for the occasional, sudden ice fall or the swallowing of a climber into a crevasse. Williams' article would appear in the April, 2015, issue of the *Seattle Met Magazine*. She would report that the backpack had belonged to a climber lost in 1986. Over the phone she described the worn fabric relics, those faded colours that were popular in the 1980s. The last effects of the climber included just one blue mitten, cologne, and a Bible. As we spoke, I felt the rough weave of the primary-blue Gore-Tex pack, its surface shedding with age like dry skin in the desert. I could feel the textured red and green nylon webbing, its soft, synthetic, frayed edges that can be melted smooth with a lighter to stop the unraveling. I could feel the coating of grit and silt that must have covered the fabric after decades under the thick glacial ice.

Ms. Williams wanted to know what I remembered of that August day we climbed Mount Baker. What did I remember of the days to follow?

Northern Lights resurfaced, the smell of summer came to mind, the smell of sweat, and dust, and pine, images I did not know I could remember appeared. As we talked, I paced and circled, holding the telephone with a shaking hand, looking out the window to see Mount Baker in 1986 in place of my snow-covered Alberta yard in 2015. Random facts rushed out of my mouth. The article was not about me, but about the others, for me it was an incomplete picture of my truth. It was not even Ian's pack, it was Steve Raschick's. I was in Plato's cave, shadows of reality begging the question, what is the real truth? And who cares about these lost objects? It's only stuff — or so I thought at the time.

While talking about those days on Mount Baker that evening, I circled my kitchen island, the phone pressed against my ear, my head filling with swirling pictures. Memories are more Rorschach than Instagram. Each time a picture or story is replayed a modified version emerges in the retelling — real truth is ephemeral. Looking back through the dust of time, I wasn't sure how much I remembered. Our conversation released vapors of my past which would have sounded like a rush of wind through tall grass had my memories been audible.

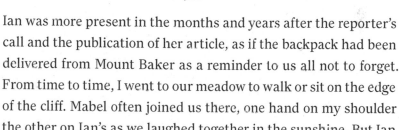

Ian was more present in the months and years after the reporter's call and the publication of her article, as if the backpack had been delivered from Mount Baker as a reminder to us all not to forget. From time to time, I went to our meadow to walk or sit on the edge of the cliff. Mabel often joined us there, one hand on my shoulder the other on Ian's as we laughed together in the sunshine. But Ian did not haunt my dreams as he had right after the avalanche, and as I began to open boxes of letters, photos, and news clippings from the past it was easy to put them back and close the lids. I realized that although some memories are hard to relive, and can sometimes still bring me to tears, having made peace with Mabel gave me an equilibrium I didn't have before. Although I may stumble from time to time, I recover more quickly. Most importantly, I remembered the joys and adventures we shared. No death can erase these past experiences.

As an homage to my past mountaineering, I took a trip in October, 2017, to Abbot Hut in British Columbia. Late fall is called the shoulder season. Neither summer nor winter, it sits between high tourist seasons. I was reminded why we feel compelled to go to high places, why Ian and I were compelled to climb Mount Baker. The same North Face backpack, now over thirty years old, still worked just fine.

In the communal journal at Abbot Hut were the following passages that tell stories of the siren call of the summit.

What a deadly place. Worth every painful step, feeling grateful and humbled by this awe-inspiring place, wrote Andrew.

Thank you for making me feel so small and so full of life, Hannah squeezed in on a line between two other entries.

It's tough to worry about much in a place this majestic, commented Kelsy.

One step forward, two steps backward on the scree, but we made it to the top despite the math, Andrew and Natashsa remarked.

The Abbot Hut trip reconnected me to my past, a reminder of steep snowy slopes. My jacket snapped like a sail in the gusty wind, and sharp snow pelted my face. I was thankful it was not a wetting rain. The fundamentals of mountaineering remain constant: preparation, experience, strength, balance, companions, and chance determine the mountain experience. The first half of the hike is always up, the variance being long and gentle or short and steep. The path to Abbot Hut is steep, with the scree slope ascent a slippery jumble of loose stones the final challenge. Conversations are always the same on the tough road up with loaded packs. Food, weather, route, and gear are the topics of choice.

"How much does your pack weigh?" a novice mountaineer asks.

"Have you tried your new food dehydrator?" a more experienced mountaineer asks. These are more modern times and yet the principles remain the same: you must know exactly how much your pack weighs, and be committed enough to the sport to be willing to invest significant time and money in preparation.

There are newer fabrics and gear in different seasonal colours, some bright pink and fluorescent green. Hiking poles to lend balance and strength on less treacherous terrain were not de rigueur until late in the twentieth century. On steep, snowy slopes the ice axe is still the go-to implement, insurance against slipping to a certain death if footing is lost above a crevasse. An arrest — digging the ice axe into the snow-pack — is still the technique to use if you don't want to slide off the slope into a deadly crevasse. I dragged Ian's old ice axe, still among my closet artifacts, up to Abbot Hut, the dings and rust on the head and taped-up, tattered handle telling the stories of prior peaks.

"No offense, but your ice axe looks like it came from a horror movie," a fellow Abbot Hut hiker remarked.

I just smiled, saying to myself, "You have no idea."

Cellular phones, which we did not have in the mid-eighties, still don't work in many alpine environments, except on the occasional summit. Even satellite phones have difficulty in steep terrain. Many alpinists look down their noses at those who expect cell service while hiking or climbing, while surreptitiously checking for signals on promising peaks. It was almost night when we arrived at Abbot Hut. There was a weak signal on the Alberta side of the summit, resulting in a line of cell phones propped up on the glass window that gathered sweat against the alpine cold outside. Climbers waited in the dark hut to capture an intermittent signal. There was no source of light and, due to a propane malfunction, heat came only from the wood stove. But for that ghostly row of cell phones, the alpine hut could have been transported here from the distant past.

I cannot talk about Abbot Hut without describing the bathroom. Bathrooms and their views continue to be another favorite topic of discussion among hikers. Abbot Hut is a ten out of ten in terms of bathroom views, my opinion based on having peed and pooed in countless remote and beautiful locations, always mindful of sanitation, whether protecting lakes or mountains, careful to leave only footprints and no toilet paper. The Abbot Hut bathroom, reportedly built by John Harrop, is "a loo with a view, a pretty place to poo," indeed stunning. For those who are in the habit of ranking bathroom locations (it's a thing), this particular bathroom is worth the climb.

The trek from the hut to the bathroom follows a four-foot wide stone walkway along the side of the small stone building; there is a precipice on one side, but no railing; then a path about twenty feet long leads up a ridge to the bathroom. This structure is cabled into the rocks. That night, in a blizzard, with a headlamp, the simple bathroom break felt like an expedition, the walkway and path obscured in the whiteout. We took turns, waiting in the hut by the door, one by one slowly creeping around the corner, head down, straining to see tracks in the snow, but they were quickly erased by the wind.

On the way down from Abbot Hut next morning, snow blanketed the loose stones on the steep, scree slope. Each mindful step demanded all my attention, one foot at a time to be sure of no slips, don't give gravity the upper hand. I felt just like one of the super-old patients navigating my clinic hallway, all concentration needed for balance. Sometimes uneven gravel from pea-size to melon-sized rocks cover a scree slope and you have to navigate downhill by digging heels in or use a modified sliding technique like downhill skiing. On this day the snow eclipsed the scree creating a surprise with each footfall and, on slippery sections, no one could dig a heel in for security.

One of my unfortunate companions slipped, then tumbled three full revolutions like a child barrel-rolling down a grassy hill.

She carried a full backpack, so a black eye and broken tooth were the best final compromise given the circumstances. Later another fellow hiker peeled off a five-foot ledge, letting loose his ice axe to career into my helmet from about ten feet above and fifteen feet away. He must have made a noise and out of the corner of my eye I saw the ice axe flying through the air towards my head. Somehow I had the presence of mind not to turn and look or it would have caught me right in the face. A tremendous clang as if I were on the inside of a massive, cathedral bell resonated in my head when it hit me. I stood for a moment, very still, before understanding that I was unharmed. First of all, take your own pulse; then, as I turned to the fallen climber, I was able to assist him. As it turned out, he ripped both medial and lateral cruciate ligaments in one of his knees. Abbot Hut was not the territory of death, but of broken bones, lost teeth, and wrecked knees. The more devastating dangers lurked higher, up on the glaciers hugging the peaks.

Abbot Hut drew me in again to the quiet at the top of a climb, looking down at a view one might imagine the raven has as she swoops among the peaks is still the draw. The remoteness of a place without access other than on foot. That place on the summit where almost no phones and no television can invade, where companions are all in together. If one falls, all are engaged to help. Each level of altitude and exposure poses a real risk, but with tangible rewards. A bathroom with a supreme view, strangers laughing together in the dark of a simple hut. The alpine experience cuts through to the core of being human. In the gentle aftermath of the final few kilometers, we rounded Lake O'Hara, the wind magically subsiding, the lake a reflecting pond bouncing back images of tall, triangle peaks of dark rock. Fingers of snow lined shady gullies, green pines and bright yellow larches dotted the forest below the treeline.

Our legs longed to stop, but with the end in sight all, including the injured, were happy to have done the trip. Any pilot is familiar with the term "hanger flying," which are stories pilots tell one another after the fact. Hikers and mountaineers do exactly the same thing; I call it "lodge climbing" or "lodge skiing." Experiences live on through the stories we tell. I never was in it to "bag a peak" and am now content to stay in the relative safety of non-glaciated trails, but I still enjoy my memories of more exciting outings. Just as my inner ear maintains my balance, my experience has allowed me to regain my equilibrium regardless of what life keeps throwing at me. That doesn't mean I am never knocked down, it just means that I'm able to find my strengths more and stand up again to move on.

"Mom, you're just going to make yourself sad," one of my adult daughters said one day as I pulled out the yellowed articles from my boxes of old papers and letters again.

"Not really," I replied, smiling. "I like to remember all these things that led me here." After a pause, I continued, "I feel very lucky."

WORDS CANNOT CAPTURE THE IMMENSE LOVE I HAVE
FOR MY DAUGHTERS ZOE AND MARGOT. I AM GRATEFUL
FOR ALL THE JOY THEY BRING TO MY WORLD.

fig. 7–3

THE EYES

———

the problem of hindsight

Months after the article about the Mount Baker avalanche was published, I stood on the shores of Ghost Lake to the west of Calgary, far
away from the city lights, with the sparkling dome of stars spread
out above me and dark water below, remembering the Northern
Lights and the phosphorescent tide. Ghost is named after the Ghost
River where, it is said, a ghost travels up the river valley to pick up
the skulls of fallen warriors, the perfect place for reminiscing.

The Northern Lights are common at this latitude. Aurora visits often, a haunting vapor swooping through the vivid stars that
sparkle like December snow even in the short summer months.

Cree mythology tells that Northern Lights are the spirits of the departed who are gone from this life, but are still present in the sky. The cool, northern, August nights come earlier and earlier with a sharp hint of winter. I can almost smell the snow behind the lingering late summer day.

I have two lovely daughters, Margot and Zoe, two beautiful lives in progress, so my wishes did come true. As they've gone from high school to university, we've enjoyed conversations about topics from genetics, to plant biology, to gender studies, and social justice — the same kind of free-wheeling give and take that we had at Carleton. We've hiked the West Coast Trail in Canada and hiked out to the backcountry lodge Skoki in Alberta a number of times. Walking, running, downhill skiing, or just hanging out at home or on the deck, they are becoming wonderful friends and adults. Back then, I don't think I could have imagined that I would have two more humans in my life to love.

Along the way, I have lost four dogs to old age and ailments, a heartbreak I'll never get used to. Then, after two decades, I lost love again to divorce, which is another kind of heartbreak. It is hard when someone dies, but in some ways worse when someone chooses to leave you. I do ask myself — what about the stop repeating, repeating, repeating part? But I am, once again, exactly where I should be. A feeling I have had more persistently in these later years.

I used to think I was bad at being alone, but it turns out I just didn't realize that I spent hours alone on the cross-country ski trails in the forest and I spent hours alone with books. I have come to relish my alone time and have rarely been lonely. If you can let go of that feeling that you need someone else with you to enjoy an experience, then the world opens up to show you the fabulous experiences all around you. Everything doesn't need to be shared or captured on film to make it a memory—those solo memories held in your heart are nourishing.

As a five-year-old, I delighted in taping bugs to the vinyl kitchen floor with clear tape in order to study them in detail. Maybe the urge to write a memoir is just like that; if you can hold memories still for a moment, perhaps you can get a better look. There is no changing the past and if you give up the notion of looking for clues as to what led you to be in this exact moment and in this exact place, then you can enjoy your memories for what they are: moments captured like random bugs caught in clear tape on the kitchen floor.

My others, including my grown-up babies, my friends who have loved me over the many years, my colleagues, my tribe of siblings and constant parents, all the other others in my life in the world that have been along for the ride are the reason it's actually been a pleasure to delve back into my story. I have been solo and duo and solo, but never alone. Whether or not my grief has written my life, I believe I would inevitably have ended up exactly in this place at this time.

My story has been punctuated by kindness. Once you learn to put your head up to look for it, kindness from others is all around, kindness that is also yours to give. Holding a door, touching an arm, driving your kids to work, giving your significant others and your plus-one (if you have one) a hand, and hugging your dog are all free. Kindnesses are a simple bright spot in the day, but some—like Doctor Parsons's quiet kindness to me in the hallway outside the cadaver lab—last a lifetime. At a funeral I attended recently, a relative said that the loss of her loved one reminded her,

"Don't be so hard on yourself." We are not robots; our cracks and damage let the light in, like the imperfections in a Navajo rug; our connections are made possible by shared sorrows, and by sharing our sorrows collectively we make our burdens lighter. At a traditional western funeral, one single person is not assigned to carry the coffin. It takes a team. Ian's father Paul was prophetic in his choice of Dylan Thomas for his funeral reading: *Though lovers be lost, love shall not.*

I always thought that this line only referred to my lost lover, but it turns out there's a ton of love beyond romantic love. If romantic love is again in my future, that would be wonderful, but I'm a whole person without it and that feels great. I am a straight-up success, while far from perfect. After all these years, I still step, rest, step, rest, reassess, revise, repeat, repeat, repeat.

Remember to get soap in your ear, walk too athletically, look to actual, real living people around you for role models, forget the air-brushed fakery the media is trying to trick you into believing is something to aspire to, and remember all the alive others who love you, including your pets, and the new others who may learn to love you. Keep your loved ones who have died — humans and animals — in your heart so their memories can lift you up. Lie in the dirt, smush your hands into paint or dough, and don't be afraid *not* to do things that scare you or that you don't want to do. Feel and be the dust that is grief until you gather your strength to get up and move forward. Remember, you cannot change chance, but you can change choice. Find the comforting side of grief because once it's part of you, it's there forever as Mabel is part of me.

I still carry Ian's last objects with me, wherever I move:

Ice Axe (looks like it came from a "horror movie", still useful)

Ice Hammer (used only once by me)

Boxes of Letters (still a pleasure to read)

Red Plaid Shirt (still fits, makes me happy)

Photos (full of joy)

Red Sweater (reminds me of both Ian and Paul)

Godel, Escher, Bach Book (dog-eared exploration of
*   fascinating ideas)*

A love of good debates & the lessons of grief

Ian is forever in my heart, and his last objects do give me the joy of remembering our life together. I hear Ian's protest—the problem of hindsight. I am well aware there was no guarantee of what would have happened if I could have prevented him from climbing Mount Baker that day, or if I had known that he would choose the Roman Wall route, and known it was dangerous, if I could have talked him out of it anyway. Who knows how long we would have been together, and if he hadn't died; would I still have my cherished daughters? Who knows? So yes, all our lives might appear to be heading in a certain direction, but who's to say for sure what's in the future. Looking back, I know my memories and experiences colour even my reading of old letters and articles—so who knows what all of it would have led to if the outcome had been different. We never had a chance to find out what would have happened, and I have made my peace with that. What I do know is that loving Ian and losing him was a gift that shaped who I am now. A gift that I would be a fool to give back if I had the cosmic chance.

On a day in June, our shared birthday month, Jenny and I met at a Carleton College reunion. We went for a walk in the arboretum. It was another timeless, warm, June night that held the promise of the coming summer. A light breeze ruffled the green leaves that arched above us over the dirt path. We found a fallen log, and sat together under the trees, two old friends, side by side.

"I feel like we're Pooh and Piglet in the Hundred Acre Wood." I paused, then continued, "But I am not sure who is Pooh and who is Piglet."

Jenny smiled. "What matters is that we'll be friends forever."

AFTERWORD

———

Over thirty-six years passed between the last time I spoke to Tommy Waller and our next conversation. Our life stories intersected for a few days in August, 1986, then diverged for almost three decades before the same reporter called both of us for the story in *Seattle Met Magazine* about the found backpack. I finally contacted him and during a phone call he described his memories of that day and the days, months, and years that followed. Our life trajectories were very different, yet our experiences very similar. Listening to Tommy's voice as he described the vivid scenes of his experience, surviving to tell of a massive avalanche, was unexpectedly comforting to me in the familiar feelings I have known. I am grateful that Tommy is willing to share his experiences and thankful to know that he is still in touch with Kurt Petellin, the other rescued climber.

Tommy told me that his experience of the avalanche was timeless blackness, then the ice and snow trying to crush him to the size of a soccer ball and smaller. Once everything stopped, as I listened to him, I could hear the silence he described when he was pinned to the mountain his blood spilling out, facing out from the snowy slope towards the beauty of the mountains on the horizon.

"Suddenly...I opened my eyes and saw a red splash on the ice before me. Then I looked up into what could at that time have been a look into Heaven to me. The softly sunlit peaks of the northern Washington and British Columbian Cascades were touched tenderly by the sunrise and I knew I was alive."

All these words are in service to our grief for our loved ones we have lost. Their memories are a blessing.

APPENDIX

Ian Kraabel Memorial Prize in History

Established in 1987 by the classmates and friends of Ian Kraabel, '85, who died in an avalanche on Mount Baker in the summer of 1986, this award honors Ian's unusual intensity, originality, and athletic ability. The Ian Kraabel Memorial Prize in History is awarded each year by the department to the senior History major who best reflects Ian's personal qualities and his desire to pursue understanding and knowledge.

Contact Carleton College at +1 507-222-4000 and ask to speak with the Chair of the History Department.

In response to one of Ian's friends: yes, it is possible to add to Ian's fund on the Giving website; via phone (507) 222-4200 or (800) 492-2275; by email: giving@carleton.edu; or by mail: Carleton College Development Office, 1 N College St, Northfield, MN 55057. If you select the online option, please indicate any amount and designate in the "Additional Instructions" box (see bottom of on-line form) that your gift is for the Ian Kraabel Memorial Prize in History. As a designated gift, it is not included in your Alumni class total.

Kraabel Prize Recipients

2023	Raine Bernhard
2022	Oliver Jacobs
2021	Alex Chertoff
2020	Anna Francesca Lauriello
2019	Ezra Sergent-Leventhal
2018	Lydia Symchych
2017	Seth Hanselman
2016	Keelin Davis
2015	Marlise Williams
2014	In Taek Hong
2013	Eli Adelman
2012	Callie Millington and Lily VanderStaay
2011	Mark Olson
2010	Daniel Curmé
2009	Ryan Oto
2008	Benjamin C. Egerman
2007	Jacob Greenberg
2006	Dominique (Nikki) Johnson
2005	Katherine (Katie) Lee Thompson Newell and Jenny Clare Freed
2004	Brett Landis
2003	Karen Joy Fricke
2002	Margaret Lee
2001	Ezra Davidson
2000	Kirsten Martens
1999	Melanie Wood
1998	Michele Nichols and Nicholas (Nick) Mark
1997	Matthew Spohn
1996	Franklin Oliver
1995	Christopher (Kit) Condill
1994	Kristin Olbertson
1993	Abigail Gillmor
1992	Etelka Lehoczky
1991	James Swartout
1990	Michael Suk
1989	Thomas Lekan
1988	Fred Nash
1987	first recipient, Humphrey Costello

ACKNOWLEDGMENTS

To my friends and family (including dogs) who are mentioned in my manuscript, I am forever in debt for your love and support. For my Carleton, med school, and residency colleagues and so many teachers and professors in my life who are not mentioned due to the constraints of writing a memoir, thank you to all of you; I am thankful for the hundreds of helping hands (and paws) that have held me up in my darkest times and shared in the joy of the better times.

This book would not exist without the support of my writing group led by Sharon Butala and the members of that group who meet regularly. I have also been inspired and encouraged by mentors in writing conferences and courses including Mary Collins (Yale) and Diane Schoemperlen (Humber) who helped me shape the manuscript. I am indebted to Harry Patz and Tommy Waller who were open to talking to me decades later about the events of the day and the aftermath. NeWest Press is a wonderful fit for this manuscript, with my editor Merrill Distad, Production Coordinator Meredith Thompson, and General Manager Matt Bowes giving great guidance in the publishing process.

Ellen Anderson Penno immigrated to Calgary, Alberta in 1997 for a refractive surgery fellowship with world renowned Dr. Howard Gimbel, subsequently earning Canadian citizenship and starting a clinical practice serving Calgarians since 2004. In 2015 a backpack belonging to a climber killed in an avalanche in 1986 emerged from a glacier at the base of Mount Baker; the second climber lost that day was her first love and mountain guide Ian Kraabel. That find launched her into writing her memoir. In the process, she attended writing workshops from Humber College in Toronto, to Harvard Medical Writers Conference and two years at the Yale

Summer Writers' Workshop. She earned a Graduate Certificate in Creative Writing from Humber College and joined a writers' group with Sharon Butala and other local authors. She holds a Graduate Certificate in Narrative Medicine, Columbia University, NYC.

She enjoys spending time walking on local trails with her adult daughters and dog pal Ed. A former Minnesotan, she loves spending time on the water paddleboarding and kayaking. In addition to her Gimbel Eye Centre fellowship and Graduate Certificate, she earned a BA from Carleton College, Northfield MN, an MD and MS from the University of Minnesota, Minneapolis MN, rotating surgical internship at Hennepin County Hospital, Minneapolis, ophthalmology residency at the Mayo Clinic, Rochester MN, and a *Guinness Book of World Records* certificate for participating in the longest indoor soccer match in 2012 organized by Martin Parnell to raise money for *Right to Play* charity.

———

This book was typeset in Family, designed by Kris Sowersby and published by Klim Type Foundry. The script typeface is IM Fell, designed by Igino Mariniand and published by Google. The sans serif is Knockout, designed by Jonathan Hoefler and published by Hoefler & Co.

———